Do Brilliantly

KS3 English

National Tests

Alan Coleby
Kate Frost

Series Editor: Jayne de Courcy

Published by HarperCollins*Publishers* Ltd
77–85 Fulham Palace Road
London W6 8JB

www.**Collins**Education.com
On-line support for schools and colleges

First published 2001

ISBN 0 00 711210 6

British Library Cataloguing in Publication Data
A catalogue record for this book is available from the British Library

Edited by Steve Attmore
Production by Kathryn Botterill
Design by Gecko Limited
Cover design by Susi Martin-Taylor
Printed and bound by Martins the Printers, Berwick upon Tweed

Acknowledgements
The Authors and Publishers are grateful to the following for permission to reproduce copyright material:
The Harvill Press for extract from *Walk a Lonely Road* by Joyce Stranger; extract from *Three Singles to Adventure* by Gerald Durrell © Gerald Durrell 1954; *The Guardian* for article 'Driven crazy' by Adrian Davies, 23 August 1989; Colin Elgie, illustrator, for permission to reproduce 'The Ultimate Nightmare'.

Illustrations
Nigel Luckhurst for the photographs on page 5.

Every effort has been made to contact the holders of copyright material, but if any have been inadvertently overlooked, the Publishers will be pleased to make the necessary arrangements at the first opportunity.

You might also like to visit:
www.**fire**and**water**.co.uk
The book lover's website

Contents

When is the Test?

You will sit your English National Test in May of Year 9. Your teacher will give you the exact dates.

What does the Test cover?

The English curriculum is divided into three Attainment Targets:

En1 Speaking and Listening
En2 Reading
En3 Writing

The Test covers Reading and Writing.

How many papers are there?

There are two Test papers. Paper 1 tests your Reading and Writing.
Paper 2 tests you on the Shakespeare play you have studied in class.

Paper 1
You are required to:
A Read an extract from a novel, short story, biography or autobiography and answer questions on it.
B Read a media text – like a leaflet or a newspaper extract – or a poem, and answer questions on it.
C Write something about a topic that is related to the texts that you read in the first two sections of the paper.

Paper 2
Paper 2 tests you on the Shakespeare play that you have studied in class.

Almost all students sit the same Test papers, but your school may decide that you should sit an extension paper by which Level 8 and exceptional performance can be achieved.

There is not a separate test for spelling, punctuation and grammar, but your marks in Paper 1 Section C (Writing) and Paper 2 do take account of your spelling, punctuation and grammar.

What is a good grade?

By the end of Key Stage 3, most pupils are between levels 3 and 7. A typical 14 year old will achieve a level 5 or 6 in their National Test.

Exceptional performance ●	} considerably better than the expected level
Level 8 ●	
Level 7 ●	} better than the expected level
Level 6 ●	} expected level for 14 year olds
Level 5 ●	
Level 4 ●	
Level 3 ●	} working towards the expected level
Level 2 ●	
Level 1 ●	
Age **14 years**	

How this book can help boost your Test result

1 Two chances to practise Paper 1 – practice makes perfect

This book contains a complete Paper 1 and a complete Paper 2. It also contains an **additional** Paper 1. This gives you **two chances** to practise answering the type of reading and writing questions you will meet on Paper 1.

2 The set scenes for all three Shakespeare plays – yours is there!

Three plays are set each year and you will have studied one of them. Two scenes from each play are set for detailed study. In the Test (Paper 2), you will be asked to answer a question on one of the scenes.

This book contains **questions on both scenes from all three plays**. This means you can practise answering questions on the play – and the scenes – that are relevant to you.

3 Detailed Answers and Tutorials – to assess your level

Detailed guidance explains how to mark each of your answers so that you can decide which level it would be awarded.

Extracts from sample answers at each level are included to provide extra help in assessing your own answers.

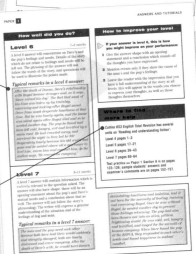

4 How to boost your grade – inside help from the experts

The authors are both KS3 English National Test examiners. In the Answers and Tutorials section they give you advice on how you can improve your answers – and so boost your grade.

This section also refers you to the relevant units of *Collins KS3 English Total Revision* for detailed help in developing particular skills.

5 Practise working under Test conditions

- Choose somewhere quiet to work while you are doing the Test.
- Get used to working under timed conditions. Don't spend more than the amount of time you will be allowed in the Test: 1 hour 30 minutes for Paper 1 (plus 15 minutes reading time) and 1 hour 15 minutes for Paper 2.

- Leave time to check your answers carefully within the time allowed.
- Do Paper 1 and Paper 2 on separate days.

If you use this book properly, it will give you the best possible preparation for your actual Test – and help you achieve your best Test score.

How to tackle your Test papers

PAPER 1

Paper 1 is divided into three sections: A, B and C.

Sections A and B

Section A

This is a test of reading. It always consists of a narrative passage – that is, a text that tells a story, true or imagined.

The two questions which follow this passage are designed to test how well you have understood the reading passage. One of these questions is worth 11 marks, and, therefore, needs as full an answer as possible; the other, shorter question, is worth only 6 marks.

Section B

This is also a test of reading.

The material in Section B varies in form. It is usually a newspaper or magazine article or an advertisement (these are called 'media texts') but it could be a poem or any kind of non-fiction text listed in the National Curriculum: leaflets, diaries, letters or travel writing. These kinds of passage often include photographs, graphs, lists, diagrams, or tables of figures. The important point is to read the text thoroughly and carefully take in all the information you are given, whatever its form.

The text is followed by one question worth 11 marks which tests your understanding of it.

Reading time

Fifteen minutes are allowed for reading passages A and B before you are permitted to write your answers. Make the best use of this time by reading both passages thoroughly and then, after noticing what the questions ask you about each passage, make notes on the inside cover of the answer booklet.

Prompts

Each question usually has two or more 'prompts' printed underneath it: these are suggestions about which points you can develop in answer to the question. A good idea, after your first reading, is to look back at the passage and note – or mark with a pencil – which parts are relevant to these prompts and, therefore, to the question.

Quotation

The questions usually advise you to refer to words and phrases from the passage to support the ideas you put in your answers. This means that you might give quotations from the passage. Quotations are words and phrases or whole sentences copied from the passage. You must remember to put inverted commas in front of, and after, the words you copy.

There are two things to remember about using a quotation. First, do not make it too long, usually no longer than a sentence. Secondly, do not just pick out any phrase or sentence, but make it refer to the ideas which you have expressed in your own words in your answer.

Remember that when examiners mark answers to the questions in Sections A and B, they do not mark writing style, spelling, punctuation, grammar, paragraphing or handwriting: they are concerned only with how well you have understood each passage.

Section C

This is a test of writing and you have to write on one of three subjects that you are given. One of these three will be a story, one a 'discursive' essay (you write about ideas, or argue a point of view) and one a description or explanation (you write about what an object, event or place looks like, or write about how you do something or how something works). This section is worth 33 marks.

You will be marked on how interesting your ideas are *and* how you express them: style, paragraphing, spelling, punctuation, grammar and handwriting. You need to write as thoughtfully and carefully as possible and check through your writing when you have finished. You need to plan it paragraph by paragraph, and then write it as accurately as you can.

The whole paper

1 hour 30 minutes is allowed for writing answers to Paper 1. You will get the most marks if you spend the amount of time suggested on the front of the question paper on each section:

Section A: 30 minutes; Section B: 20 minutes; Section C: 35 minutes.

This leaves five minutes for checking through at the end.

Remember that Sections A and B added together are worth 28 marks, and that Section C is worth 33 marks. Therefore, Section C is worth more than the rest of the paper put together, and so whatever you do, do not leave yourself short of time for Section C.

PAPER 2

This paper lasts 1 hour 15 minutes, with no time for reading. At the start, you are given three booklets. The first contains the questions, and the second is for your answers. The third one contains the scenes set from each play, which is why you do not need to take a copy of the play into the Test. (To answer the questions in this book, you will, of course, need your own text.)

Three plays are set each year. You will have studied one of them, and you will have been told which two particular scenes there will be questions on. There will be six questions altogether on Paper 2, two of which will be on the play you have studied. You must answer one of these two questions.

Remember that two types of mark are awarded for the answer to each question on this paper: one for understanding and one for writing skills. Therefore, in your answer you need to show that you understand each aspect of the scene (plot, character, meaning and language) and can make your knowledge relevant to the question. You must also be careful to write accurately (spelling, punctuation, grammar) and in well-organised paragraphs.

A number of 'prompts', usually about four, are placed underneath the main question, which will always be in bold print. It is best to base your answer on these prompts, writing a few paragraphs on each in turn.

Shakespeare questions are of three types. First, there is the 'critical discussion' question which will ask about aspects of plot, character, meaning or language in the scene. Secondly, the 'empathetic' question asks you to imagine you are one of the characters and to write as if you are that person. Thirdly, you may be asked to imagine that you are directing what happens on the stage in a scene, and so you must write what you would tell the actors to do.

The first of the types of question, 'critical discussion', is the most frequently set. Remember that in your answer to such a question you must include quotations. Do not make these quotations too long (two or three lines at the most) and make them refer clearly to the ideas which you express in your own words.

With the second of these types of question, it is important to show that you know what all the other characters think, do and say, as well as concentrating on your particular character.

With the third of these types of question, it is important to show your knowledge of the characters, meaning and language of the scene, as well as talking about stage effects and actions.

How to calculate your level

In the Answers and Tutorials, the 'How well did you do?' section gives an example of each type of answer for each level. For this a range of marks is given.

First you need to decide which level your answer is at. Then you have to give yourself a mark from within the range given. You need to decide, for example, whether your answer is a good level 5 (in which case you would award yourself the top mark possible), or whether it is a poor level 5 (in which case you would award yourself the mark at the bottom of the range).

When you have given yourself a mark for each question in Paper 1 and Paper 2 (remembering that in Paper 2 there are two *types* of mark for each question), add them up to get your total mark.

Below is a table showing what your total mark means in terms of levels:

Marks	Level
25–39	4
40–55	5
56–73	6
74–99	7

ENGLISH TEST PAPER ①

Reading and Writing

Section A

Read the following story. Then answer all the questions which follow it.

The story tells how Dave Martin, a police dog handler, loses his dog, Royal, killed while on duty. Royal is replaced by an Alsatian pup, which has been abandoned near a busy main road.

Dave valued his dog, Royal, more than did most of the police dog handlers. His wife had been killed in a car crash only a few months ago. The house would be desolate without Royal, and the days after Donna's death would have been even more impossible. As it was, he had had the Alsatian to train and feed and exercise and groom. The dog was salvation. Its routine care helped ride the hours of grief. 5

Man and dog had gone out of the silent night into devastation. The youths were high on drugs and drink. They were yelling lunatics, knowing no bounds to violence.

The barman and the landlord had knife wounds, and another youth was badly hurt. Dave signalled and Royal leaped. The savage knife slashed his neck. Dave stormed forward, fury mastering him, as the Alsatian dropped, blood pouring from him. Rage 10 carried the man through the evening, carried him through the arrests, carried him through the routine details.

Later that night, he went back for his dog. The landlord had tidied up. Royal lay on a clean sheet. Dave Martin looked down and passion died. It was replaced by a sense of total loss. 15

The pup had been tied to a litter bin in a lay-by on a busy main road by a heartless man who no longer wanted him. He was cold, wet and terrified by the speeding cars and lorries that hurtled along the road. As soon as he had bitten through the rope, he crept into a field and crouched under a hedge, nose on paws, eyes forlorn. He shivered. He gathered his courage at dusk when the traffic eased, and crawled into a dilapidated 20 shed that kept off some of the rain. He lived through the terrifying dark, which was criss-crossed by inexplicable lights that flashed over him. His ears were outraged by continuous noise. Dawn brought a sunny sky, and a bitter wind. The pup padded outside. His world had ended. Everything familiar had vanished.

The air was cold, chilling his sodden fur. The wintry sun had little warmth. There was 25 hunger, an empty tormenting ache. Worst of all, aloneness was total terror. He was driven by a compelling need for someone to stroke him and pet him and praise him, some creature with warmth in its body against which he could curl and rest. He craved for company.

Dave heard about the pup from Bess Taylor when he went into the canteen. She knew 30 how much he missed Royal. She guessed he would be anxious to have another dog quickly. 'There's a pup at the RSPCA,' she said. 'An Alsatian.'

'Wild as they come,' one of the other policemen said. 'Reckon he'd have a finger off as soon as look at you.'

Dave listened. A dog. An Alsatian. An Alsatian that had been abandoned, that nobody wanted, that might make a police dog. He couldn't wait to finish his shift. A dog that would be his. A dog to replace Royal, to banish isolation, to liven the silent house. Excitement built in him, and he longed to get home.   35

At last came release. Dave changed out of uniform and drove round to see Alice, from the RSPCA. Once indoors, the pup watched him, wary.   40

'Have you any plans for him?' Dave asked. Alice shook her head.

Dave looked at the pup. He held his head well, his ears, alert and sensitive, moving as Dave or Alice spoke, and he seemed to listen intently. A noise outside drove him to the window, eager to investigate. Dave had heard nothing. The pup was alert. He'd be splendid on patrol.   45

Dave flicked his fingers. The Alsatian ran back to the hearth rug and jumped at him, responding eagerly to the masculine smell. Dave knelt and the little animal sniffed at him, learning every detail, knowing without need of words that this man had lived with another dog. Royal's scent still lingered on Dave's clothes.

'How old is he?' Dave asked. 'About six months?'   50

'More than seven, I'd say,' Alice answered. 'He's not been running loose that long, but he's in need of proper nourishment. He's thin but not starvation-thin. From his size, I'd guess he's only had table scraps.'

'Can I take him soon?' Dave asked, and Alice nodded.

He had already adopted the dog; had looked ahead to the coming years, to the feel of the animal beside him, lightening patrol duties; to the weeks of training; to the knowledge that he need not wait for a replacement. He needed the pup. He bent to caress it. The stroking hand was firm and masculine.   55

'He trusts you,' Alice said. The pup never leaned against her. 'But suppose the sergeant decides he isn't suitable? What then?'   60

The pup put his head on Dave's knee. When Dave stood, the pup stood too, looking anxiously. Dave thrust the thought from him. He did not want any dog. He wanted this dog, now.

'I'll face that when I have to,' Dave said. 'This is my dog.' He flicked his fingers and the pup licked his hand.   65

'He wouldn't do that for me,' Alice said. She hoped the sergeant would agree. The pup was following Dave to the door, wanting to go with the man, already belonging.

'What will you call him?' Alice asked. 'I call him Blackie, but that's too soft for a police dog.'

Dave looked down. It was hard to decide. Janus? Simba? Tam? None of them fitted. Rex? The pup was never going to be kingly.   70

He thought of Royal, who needed an epitaph. 'I'll call him Avenger,' he said. The pup wagged his tail. So long as he had a name and a master to call his name, he did not care.

From 'Walk a Lonely Road' by Joyce Stranger

Section A

Answer the following questions.

1   **Explain why the man and the pup need each other.**

In your answer you should comment on:

*   Dave's feelings about Royal after his wife had died;

*   Dave's need for another dog after he had lost Royal;

*   the pup's feelings after he had been abandoned.

11 marks

2   **Describe how the pup shows his affection for Dave.**

In your answer you should comment on:

*   the things the pup does with Dave;

*   the reasons why he does these things.

6 marks

Section B

Read the piece entitled FRAME A FUTURE FOR CHILDREN.

This is an advertisement placed in a local newspaper. It is trying to persuade people to become foster parents.

Now answer question 3. Refer to words and phrases in the advertisement to support your ideas.

3   **How does the article try to persuade the readers to become foster parents?**

In your answer you should comment on:

*   the information given about the children, both the content and the order in which it is arranged;

*   the way the words and layout are used to get the reader interested;

*   whether you think the leaflet will succeed in attracting some enquiries.

11 marks

FOR CHILDREN

FRAME A FUTURE

ALISON

Alison is a lively and talkative 13 year old who enjoys adult company and praise for her achievements. She enjoys cycling, swimming and discos and is doing well at school. As with all teenagers, Alison can be argumentative but she is genuinely eager to please and be helpful and this makes her a rewarding young person to care for.

Foster carers are required to provide Alison with a family life until she is able to live independently. She wants to stay in the Leytonshire area in order to keep in contact with her own family, which is still very important to her. Her foster carers could be experienced parents whose own children have grown up or a single female carer.

We will provide some training, ongoing advice and support and a weekly allowance to cover the cost of looking after Alison.

LAZLO

Lazlo is an attractive, quiet 14-year-old boy whose hobbies are reading and playing video games. He likes company but hates being the centre of attention. He can sometimes be withdrawn and needs delicate handling; relationships with peers are difficult for him, though he does have one firm friend at his local school, with whom he would like to stay in touch.

Lazlo is also anxious to remain in contact with relatives in Leytonshire, though he has lost both his parents. His elderly aunt and uncle provide a link with his Eastern European roots which he feels he needs.

Are there any foster carers out there with the skills and patience to nurture Lazlo into adulthood? He needs an ordered environment with experienced parents; a family with younger children may be good for him.

IF YOU ARE INTERESTED AND MAY BE ABLE TO HELP THESE YOUNG PEOPLE, OR OTHERS LIKE THEM — please telephone Lucy or Steve on Leyton (01228) 874635587 for more information.

Leytonshire County Council Social Services

Section C

This section is a test of your ability to write clearly and accurately in your own style using:

* *paragraphs;*

* *a range of sentence structures and vocabulary;*

* *correct spelling and punctuation.*

Aim to write about two pages of your answer booklet.

You may use notepaper to help you plan your answer.

Whichever task you choose, your writing can be true or imaginary.

Choose ONE of the following:

4   EITHER

(a) **Write about an incident which ended in disappointment.**

You could write about:

* looking forward to the incident;

* what you hoped for during it or after it;

* how and why it did not go as you expected;

* your feelings after it was over.

OR

(b) **Suppose that you are writing the story of your childhood and have reached a part where you wish to deal with your relationships with each member of your family OR your neighbours. Write this part.**

In your writing you could comment on:

* how each person behaves towards you;

* how you behave towards each person;

* if you like each person and why.

OR

(c) **What impressions of family life are given by television serials?**

In your writing you could comment on:

* particular programmes, whether they are true to life;

* how many families they are built upon.

33 marks

Answers and Tutorials
Paper 1
Sections A and B

HOW TO MARK YOUR ANSWERS

How well did you do?

For each question, there is a description of the **type of answer** that Test Examiners would expect to see at each level. Also included are examples of **typical remarks** that students would be likely to include at each level.

Read through each of your answers several times to see if you can match it up to the level where it seems to fit best.

If you are unsure, ask someone you can trust – a relative or friend – to help you.

How to improve your level

Once you have decided what level your answer is, look at the column headed 'How to improve your level'. This suggests what you need to do to improve your skills so that you can give a better answer next time – and achieve a higher level.

Where to find more help

This section includes detailed references to *Collins KS3 English Total Revision*. Whichever level you are working at in your reading, this book will help you to develop the skills you need.

Paper 1
Section A Question 1

How well did you do?	How to improve your level

Level 4   *3–4 marks*

Questions which follow a story are to test *understanding* of it. A level 4 answer will show only that the events of the story are known, not that they have been really understood. Therefore, when there is a question, such as this, about particular aspects of a story, a level 4 answer will go to the relevant part, but will then just follow the story and forget what the question asked for.

Typical remarks in a level 4 answer:

Dave had feelings for Royal because Dave's wife died in a car crash a few months back, so Dave needed Royal. Dave needed another dog after Royal had died at the pub. He was bored after Royal had died. His friends in the canteen told him there was an Alsatian pup at the RSPCA.

▶ **If your answer is *level 4*, this is how you might improve on your performance:**

1 Show that you understand how the events in the story are caused: do not just state them.

2 Keep trying to think of your own words to express your ideas.

3 Do not write as if you are telling a story. Keep looking at what the question asks for.

Level 5   *5–6 marks*

A level 5 answer will mention the death of the wife, the loss of Royal and the abandoning of the pup. It will not, however, concentrate on Dave's and the pup's feelings, or their causes. The phrasing of the original passage will be followed.

Typical remarks in a level 5 answer:

Dave's wife had been killed in a car crash a few months ago. Dave had no-one to stay with except his dog, Royal. Without his dog, the house would have been desolate. Dave cared about his dog a lot. His care helped ride the hours of grief and when Royal died, Dave needed another dog. The pup was wet and terrified by the speeding cars and lorries. He crawled into a field and later into a shed, but he was cold and hungry and alone.

▶ **If your answer is *level 5*, this is how you might improve on your performance:**

1 Mention the events of the story if you must, but show how they *caused* the man's and the pup's feelings.

2 You will show that you understand the point of the story, if you constantly try to search for your own words to explain it.

3 Without wandering off the point, add your own thoughts to show that you understand and can sympathise with Dave's and the pup's feelings.

How well did you do?

Level 6
7–8 marks

A level 6 answer will concentrate on Dave's and the pup's feelings and needs. Details of the story which do not relate to feelings and needs will be left out. The phrasing of the answer will not follow the words of the story, and quotations will be used to illustrate the points made.

Typical remarks in a level 6 answer:

After the death of Donna, Dave's relationship with Royal became stronger and, as it says, 'Dave valued his dog'. The fact that most of his time was taken up by training, exercising and looking after Royal saved Dave from much desperate loneliness at that time. But he was lonely again, and the house was silent again after Royal died and so he needed another dog. The pup he found had been left cold, hungry, wet and terrified by a main road. He had crawled away, and survived the night in fear, but he felt desperately lonely because his old world had gone and he needed above all a newcomer to feed him, warm him and comfort him. As the author says, 'He craved for company.'

Level 7
9–11 marks

A level 7 answer will contain information which is *entirely* relevant to the question asked. The answer will also have shape: there will be an opening statement about the pup's and Dave's mutual needs and a conclusion about that as well. The answer will not follow the story's phraseology. The writer will express a genuine understanding of the situation and of the feelings of dog and man.

Typical remarks in a level 7 answer:

The man and the pup need each other because both have had their world suddenly and abruptly changed; both are lonely, distressed and crave company. After the death of Dave's wife, he would have known

How to improve your level

 If your answer is *level 6*, this is how you might improve on your performance:

1 Give the answer shape with an opening statement and a conclusion which rounds off the thoughts you have expressed.

2 Mention events only if they show the cause of the man's and the pup's feelings.

3 Leave the reader with the impression that you have a full understanding of the story at all levels: this will appear in the words you choose to express your thoughts, as well as those thoughts themselves.

Where to find more help

Collins KS3 English Total Revision has several units on 'Reading and understanding fiction':

Level 4 pages 1–3

Level 5 pages 17–21

Level 6 pages 39–43

Level 7 pages 60–64

Test practice on Paper 1 Section A is on pages 123–126; sample students' answers and examiner's comments are on pages 152–157.

devastating loneliness and isolation, had it not been for the necessity of feeding, training and exercising Royal. Once he was without Royal, he needed another dog to prevent those feelings returning. The pup had also been thrown out into an alien, pitiless, frightening world. He was cold, wet, hungry and terrified, and longed for the warmth of human company. When Dave found the pup at the RSPCA, they responded to each other's needs and found happiness in mutual comfort.

Paper 1
Section A Question 2

| How well did you do? | How to improve your level |

Level 4
2 marks

A level 4 answer will often follow the words of the story, which is not a good idea, except for the occasional word. It will give information from the last section of the story, but will mix what Dave did and what the pup did without showing how the pup shows affection for Dave, which is what the question asks for.

Typical remarks in a level 4 answer:

> *The pup held his head well, his ears moved as Dave or Alice spoke. He went to the window but Dave heard nothing. The Alsatian jumped at him and sniffed him and he flicked his fingers and the pup licked his hand.*

▷ **If your answer is *level 4*, this is how you might improve on your performance:**

1 Answer in your own words, and do not just follow the story.

2 See what the question exactly asks for, and give that – the pup's actions and how they show affection for Dave.

3 Do not put what Dave did – this is not asked for.

Level 5
3 marks

A level 5 answer will mainly be in the writer's own words. However, most of it will describe things the pup did, with only a little explanation of what his actions *mean*.

Typical remarks in a level 5 answer:

> *The pup listened and Dave thought he was alert. When Dave flicked his fingers, the pup ran and jumped at him and then sniffed at him. He stroked him and the pup showed he liked it. He put his head on Dave's knee, stood up with him and licked his hand.*

▷ **If your answer is *level 5*, this is how you might improve on your performance:**

1 Search through the last section – which is the part of the story where Dave and the pup meet – to make sure you have found all the things that the pup did.

2 Work out a connection between each of the pup's actions and how it proves affection for Dave – bring in what Dave does in this connection.

3 Try to include quotations from the story, using inverted commas (' '), but work these into your own sentences.

How well did you do?

Level 6

4 marks

A level 6 answer will *explain* the pup's behaviour as well as describe his actions. It will be a full, detailed answer, showing a good understanding of the developing relationship between Dave and the pup. Quotations from the passage will be used well to illustrate the points made.

Typical remarks in a level 6 answer:

> *When Dave flicked his fingers, the pup ran to him and jumped at him because he liked his manly scent. He could also smell Royal's scent on Dave's clothes as he sniffed at them. He knew that Dave understood dogs because he 'had lived with another dog'. He also liked Dave stroking him and showed his affection by putting his head on his knee and was anxious when Dave stood to go. He licked Dave's hand and followed him to the door to show that he wanted him to own him: he was 'wanting to go with the man, already belonging'.*

Level 7

5–6 marks

In a level 7 answer, all the connections between what the pup does to show affection and the reasons for his behaviour will be understood and described. The answer will display a higher degree of understanding (perception) and the writer will choose appropriate words to express this.

Typical remarks in a level 7 answer:

> *Although he had been distracted by a noise at the window, the pup ran back to Dave and jumped at him, so responding to the manly scent he will have known previously in his life. For the same reason, he loved Dave stroking him and put his head on his knee. When Dave rose to go, the pup was anxious that he would lose him and so, after licking his hand and returning Dave's gesture of physical contact, he followed him to the door.*

How to improve your level

> **If your answer is *level 6*, this is how you might improve on your performance:**

1 To get a level 6 answer you will have connected all the pup's actions with the reasons for them. Think hard about the relationship of the man and the pup, and show an understanding of every part of that relationship.

2 Think about why the pup responds to Dave more than the lady who has been looking after him. This will show an understanding which is deeper than that of most other students. Think about things from the pup's point of view, and you may be able to express an even deeper understanding – is there a connection with other parts of the story?

3 Give quotations which have an exact connection with the question; also, search your mind for the best possible word to express your understanding – not just a word which is near enough, a word you might use in conversation.

Where to find more help

Collins KS3 English Total Revision has several units on 'Reading and understanding fiction':

Level 4 pages 1–3

Level 5 pages 17–21

Level 6 pages 39–43

Level 7 pages 60–64

Test practice on Paper 1 Section A is on pages 123–126; sample students' answers and examiner's comments are on pages 152–157.

> *This demonstrated his desire to belong to him, 'wanting to go with the man, already belonging'. It was not that the pup disliked Alice, but Dave's manliness aroused a deeply-felt desire in the pup to belong.*

Paper 1
Section B Question 3

<table>
<tr><td>**How well did you do?**</td><td>**How to improve your level**</td></tr>
</table>

Level 4

3–4 marks

A level 4 answer will concentrate mainly on the facts (i.e. what the advertisement is about). It will make only one or two comments about the layout. There will not be much detail or quotation to support what is said.

Typical remarks in a level 4 answer:

> *The writers have said the nice things about the children first.*
> *Some words are in bold type to attract your attention.*
> *The layout tries to get your attention.*
> *I think the children are not always well behaved.*

▷ **If your answer is *level 4*, this is how you might improve on your performance:**

1 Make sure you answer all the prompts. Perhaps a paragraph on each.

2 When you have dealt with each point, try to find a few words from the original (a quotation) and copy it into your answer.

3 Don't be in too much hurry to get on to the next question.

Level 5

5–6 marks

A level 5 answer will include the facts *plus* generalisations about the aims of the advertisement. Some points will be made about how the reader might be persuaded, maybe linked to the pictures and some of the words.

Typical remarks in a level 5 answer:

> *The order of the writing describes the child first, what the hobbies are and then what would be good for them.*
> *The information about foster carers at the bottom is useful.*
> *My Mum would probably want to foster if she read this because she is very soft-hearted, and so am I. I don't think we could persuade my Dad, though.*

▷ **If your answer is *level 5*, this is how you might improve on your performance:**

1 Make sure you concentrate equally on all aspects of the task. Do not miss some bits out just because they seem more difficult.

2 Include relevant quotations. The best ones not only prove your points but add a bit more.

3 When you have completed your answer, read through the task again to make sure you have not missed anything vital.

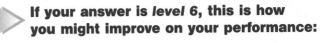

How well did you do?

Level 6
7–8 marks

In a level 6 answer the emphasis will be on the persuasive powers of the advertisement: not just *what* it says but *how* the material is presented. It will mention words used and the layout, and will give supporting quotations wherever helpful.

Typical remarks in a level 6 answer:

> *The article gives information about the children, then a paragraph about what kind of foster carers are wanted.*
> *The leaflet should attract a few enquiries because it explains that these children are nice but unlucky.*
> *The children look sweet in the pictures, which might win over a few hearts.*
> *I like the way that the writer doesn't pretend that the children are perfect. Everyone has some faults. Especially some teenagers can be difficult and these are. Alison can be 'argumentative' when she isn't doing the things she likes.*

Level 7
9–11 marks

A level 7 answer will have it all. It will be clear about the aims of the advertisement and why it is written and arranged as it is. It will analyse the content and comment on the language and the layout in detail.

Typical remarks in a level 7 answer:

> *This article plays upon the emotions of the readers in clever ways. It uses photographs of smiling children and tugs the heartstrings by explaining their unhappy circumstances. All the positive features of the children are emphasised: 'enjoys adult company and praise ... enjoys cycling, swimming and discos ... doing well at school ... genuinely eager to please'. You have to look much more closely to find the negative points: 'can be argumentative'; 'can sometimes be withdrawn'.*
>
> *The title 'frame a future' is a play on words as the headline is framing the article on two sides.*

How to improve your level

▷ **If your answer is *level* 6, this is how you might improve on your performance:**

1 Check that everything you have included is relevant to the task set. Students at this level often write longer answers than they need to and then find themselves short of time at the end.

2 If you can give an overview, as well as details, so much the better.

3 If you are asked for an opinion, do not be afraid to express one. Try to avoid the one that first springs to mind: that is likely to be the obvious one and you want yours to be special.

Where to find more help

Collins KS3 English Total Revision has several units on 'Reading and understanding non-fiction':

Level 4 pages 4–6

Level 5 pages 22–25

Level 6 pages 44–47

Level 7 pages 65–68

Test practice on Paper 1 Section B is on pages 127–128; sample students' answers and examiner's comments are on pages 158–161.

Answers and Tutorials
Paper 1
Section C

HOW TO MARK YOUR ANSWER

How well did you do?

Examiners assess students' writing according to a range of different criteria:

1 *What* you write. Examiners judge the number and quality of your ideas – your imagination and originality.

2 The *structure* of your writing – for example, how you begin and end your essay, how varied your sentence structure is, how you divide your writing into paragraphs etc.

3 Expression and style. Examiners assess your choice of words and phrases. They look at how *exact* and appropriate your words are, and how you arrange your words and phrases into sentences and paragraphs.

4 How accurate your grammar, spelling and punctuation are, and how legible your handwriting is.

In order to work out what level you would be awarded for the essay you have written, you need to read through the general assessment guidance that is given for each level. This covers all the aspects mentioned above.

Also read carefully the typical sentences that an examiner would expect to see in an essay at each level. Your sentences will obviously not be the same – but you should be able to spot whether your writing shares the same characteristics.

See if you can match your essay up to the level where it seems to fit best. If you are unsure, ask someone you can trust – a relative or friend – to help you.

How to improve your level

Once you have decided what level your writing would be awarded, look at the column headed 'How to improve your level' which is alongside.

This suggests what you need to do to improve your writing skills so that you can write a better essay next time – and achieve a higher level.

Where to find more help

This section includes detailed references to *Collins KS3 English Total Revision*. Whichever level you are working at in your writing, this book will help you to develop the skills you need.

Paper 1
Section C Question 4(a)

How well did you do?

Level 4

8–12 marks

In any kind of writing test, students love to write stories. In this question, they are asked to 'Write about an incident', and so quite a large part of it will be the story of what happened. Notice, however, that this is not the whole task in this case, because they have to describe the disappointment at the end. The 'prompts' (the extra instructions underneath the main question) say that they have to write about feelings before, during and after the incident.

A level 4 answer may deal only with the story part, and even then will not bother with dialogue (speech) or detail. The writer will not search for exact descriptive words and will often be inconsistent with tenses – that is, sometimes writing in the present tense, and sometimes in the past tense. The style may be colloquial – writing as you speak. There will be correct sentences, but punctuation and spelling may be poor because the writer has not checked his or her work.

Typical sentences from a level 4 answer:

Our teacher had suggested that we should raise some money, so we reckoned a sponsored walk would be the best way. It had all been fixed for a dozen of us to walk 20 miles on a route in the wolds, only it was harder than we thought. The weather is good and we set off at a good speed, but as we are coming down so many hills, it starts hurting my feet. I am wearing training shoes and I start to feel real sore on my heel and then my toe starts hurting. I think it's that toenail that I went to the doctor's with. It doesn't half hurt.

How to improve your level

▷ **If your answer is *level 4*, this is how you might improve on your performance:**

1 You must be consistent with your tenses. If you start with the past tense, which is usually the best choice, then keep to it. If you start with the present tense, stay with that.

2 Do not let sentences run on until they are too long and incorrect. Mix some short sentences in with the longer ones. Do not use the word 'so' to connect long phrases to try to make them into sentences: this is not correct grammar.

3 Try to choose exact words to express what you mean and do not write in the same style in which you would speak: instead of 'reckoned', 'fixed' and 'doesn't half hurt', use words like 'thought', 'arranged' and 'was very painful'.

4 Write in paragraphs and arrange them so that they follow each other logically. This helps the reader to follow your thoughts.

How well did you do?

Level 5
14–18 marks

A level 5 answer will contain more exact words; the style will not be so colloquial. Tenses will be consistent and the writing is most likely to be in the past tense. The ideas will be arranged in paragraphs according to the suggestions in the 'prompts' (the extra instructions underneath the main question). Speech may be used, because this controls the pace of the story and adds realism. Spelling and punctuation, including full stops, speech marks, commas and apostrophes, will be mostly correct, and the handwriting will be clear.

Typical sentences from a level 5 answer:

Mr Thornton, our form teacher, had suggested that we should raise some money so that the school band could go abroad in the Easter holidays.

My friends and I love playing in the band, and when he suggested an engagement at a school in Germany, we were absolutely thrilled. We hoped to raise £400, and the Head promised that if we did, the school would pay the rest. A sponsored walk seemed the best idea, and we planned a route of twenty miles on footpaths through the wolds.

'You'll never do twenty miles,' laughed Dad, when he heard of it.

'Oh yes, I will,' I replied. 'I'll just think of going to Germany, and that will focus all my efforts on finishing.'

How to improve your level

▷ **If your answer is *level 5*, this is how you might improve on your performance:**

1 Use dialogue to control the speed of the story. Make it natural and make it fit the character who speaks it.

2 Before you start, plan your writing, especially the paragraphing, so that the reader can easily follow the different stages of the action, description and thought. At special points, give descriptive detail that the reader will remember.

3 Search for precise words to give exact information or thoughts. Try to think of the most interesting way of explaining something.

4 Check spelling, punctuation and sentence construction to make sure there are no errors interrupting the fluency of your writing.

How well did you do?

Level 6

20–24 marks

Level 6 writing will genuinely interest the reader. It will include dialogue (speech) and detail. It will introduce changes of pace and will hold the reader's attention by making the detail believable. There will be a wider choice of vocabulary, carrying a range of thoughts and ideas. Sentences will be quite well constructed. Punctuation will be accurate so that it helps make the meaning clear, and all except the most difficult words will be spelled correctly.

Typical sentences from a level 6 answer:

My friends and I really wanted this sponsored walk to be a success. Mr Thornton had suggested the idea so that the school band, in which we all loved playing, could go to Germany to give a concert in the Easter holidays.

In spite of taunts that I would not make it, I was determined. I wanted so much to go to Germany. The day arrived. We set off in fine weather, chatting to each other, enjoying the scenery, and we had covered ten miles when we stopped for a packed lunch.

As we set off in the afternoon, however, I was aware of a very sore right heel. I knew this would be a blister, and I did not want to stop to apply a plaster. I persevered, driven on by a relentless ambition to succeed.

'I'm not stopping,' I muttered. 'I am going to get there, whatever happens.'

How to improve your level

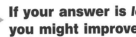

If your answer is *level 6*, this is how you might improve on your performance:

1 Make it easy for a reader to follow the rhythm of your writing by varying the length of the sentences from short and sharp, to long and detailed.

2 Find the most precise words for description. In our example of level 7 writing (page 18), 'extensive views', 'exhilarating', 'urged on', 'as a deposit', 'without attention', 'protested vehemently' and 'insisted' are precise words, which sometimes save half a sentence of less concentrated writing.

3 The end of a piece of writing must leave a sense of satisfaction in the mind of a reader. Try to make the last few sentences a satisfying conclusion by looking back or by neatly rounding off something you have been leading up to. This question asks you to explain 'your feelings after it was over'.

How well did you do?

Level 7   *26–33 marks*

All the best elements of the craft of writing will be present at this level. There will be variation in sentence structure. There will be well-planned paragraphs, realistic dialogue and use of significant detail. The words will be well chosen from a wide range of vocabulary, and will be arranged in an attractive way. Spelling and punctuation will be very accurate and handwriting will be perfectly clear.

Typical sentences from a level 7 answer:

The sponsored walk went well during the morning. The weather was fine, the extensive views across the wolds were exhilarating, and our spirits were high. Urged on by our desire to earn £400 as a deposit for the band's Easter visit to Germany, we made good time and had completed ten miles by lunchtime.
During the afternoon, I developed a sore heel. I knew it would be a blister, and decided to let it bleed without attention. Soon, however, there was a much sharper pain in my big toe. The doctor had warned me about the possibility of an ingrown toenail and had advised on the correct method of trimming the nail. The pain became so intense, that eventually I was forced to sit down and remove my shoe. Mr Thornton persuaded me to stop and go to a nearby road for a lift to the finish. I protested vehemently, but he insisted.
I felt terrible; I had a sinking feeling inside. He said my sponsors would pay for fifteen miles, but that did not help the way I was feeling. I had let the others down. I felt weak and ashamed.

Where to find more help

Collins KS3 English Total Revision has several units on 'Imaginative writing':

Level 4 pages 7–9

Level 5 pages 26–30

Level 6 pages 48–52

Level 7 pages 69–72

The unit on 'The essentials of language' (pages 101–118) explains how to improve grammar, punctuation and spelling.

Test practice on Paper 1 Section C is on page 129; sample students' answers and examiner's comments are on pages 162–180.

Paper 1
Section C Question 4(b)

How well did you do?	**How to improve your level**

Level 4
8–12 marks

A piece of writing at level 4 will contain one or two ideas. It will be organised into proper sentences, and the writer will try to use effective vocabulary. Most of the punctuation will be in the right places and quite a lot of the words will be spelled correctly. The handwriting will be fairly clear.

Typical sentences from a level 4 answer:

> *My Dad used to play football with me and my brother. It was great. He was always there for me. We used to go to this field at the back of my Gran's. She lives about half a mile away from us and after we could go for a cup of tea and she used to bake buns with cherries on. Dad didn't always win when we played, in fact sometimes I think he let us win on purpose so that we would feel good.*

> **If your answer is *level 4*, this is how you might improve on your performance:**
>
> 1 Make sure you have done exactly what the task asked you to do. There are usually extra bits of advice that it is wise to pay attention to.
>
> 2 Always organise your writing into paragraphs – making a plan before you start might help.
>
> 3 When you check through your work, have a system: make sure it all makes sense; make sure you have used the right punctuation marks to make the meaning clear; check spellings – more mistakes are made in simple words than in complicated ones because students tend not to concentrate on them as much.

Level 5
14–18 marks

At level 5, writing will be more clearly expressed than at level 4, with ideas arranged in an interesting way, probably in paragraphs. The punctuation, including commas, apostrophes and speech marks, will be mostly correct. Most of the words will be spelled correctly.

Typical sentences from a level 5 answer:

> *When my sister and I were arguing, Mum always had a way of making the peace so that neither of us got upset. I used to say, 'It's not fair. I did the washing up yesterday and the day before. It's Sandra's turn.'*
> *My Mum had an answer, 'Yes, but Sandra washed the kitchen floor yesterday and did all the cleaning at the weekend so I could go and see your Grandad in hospital.'*
> *I hope that I'll be a good mum like her one day, I really think she's great.*

> **If your answer is *level 5*, this is how you might improve on your performance:**
>
> 1 Make sure your paragraphs follow on from one another logically. The reader must be able to follow your train of thought.
>
> 2 Try to be more precise in your choice of words; avoid repeating the same words if you can; try to think of more interesting ways of explaining something.
>
> 3 When you have completed your answer, use any time left over for a thorough check: spelling, punctuation and grammar. The punctuation of any speech you have written down can be a minefield – look at it again!

How well did you do?

Level 6 — *20–24 marks*

By level 6 the piece of writing will be genuinely interesting. There will be parts that hold the reader's attention because of either the ideas themselves or because there are some cleverly used words and expressions. The punctuation will make the writing so clear that it is really reader-friendly. All except the most difficult words will be spelled correctly.

Typical sentences from a level 6 answer:

> *Although my Grandfather was quite ancient, he had the best sense of humour I have ever come across; he never laughed at us, only with us. His eyes shone with love. I remember particularly one Christmas when he was staying with us, he crept downstairs before anyone else and removed all my parents' presents and hid them. Mum and Dad (who had put all the presents under the tree, of course) daren't say anything at all, for fear of spoiling the 'Santa' surprise.*

Level 7 — *26–33 marks*

Level 7 writing will be confident and slightly out of the ordinary. It will be easy to read because the words are so well chosen and arranged in such an attractive way. The spelling and punctuation will be very accurate.

Typical sentences from a level 7 answer:

> *Then there was that detestable old stick, Great Aunt Constance. Where she bought her clothes from, goodness only knows! I am sure that kind of wardrobe is not available in any shop.*
> *'Haven't you grown!' she always used to say. It would have been a bit of a shock to her if we hadn't.*

How to improve your level

If your answer is *level 6*, this is how you might improve on your performance:

1 Take a bit of time before you start, to plan your writing. You can sometimes make it more special by arranging your paragraphs in an unusual order. Novel writers often do this.

2 An extra adjective in a description here and there, or a well-chosen adverb, can transform a piece of writing. Speech can often liven up a story, providing you do not overdo it.

3 Check everything very carefully at the end.

Where to find more help

Collins KS3 English Total Revision has several units on 'Imaginative writing':

Level 4 pages 7–9

Level 5 pages 26–30

Level 6 pages 48–52

Level 7 pages 69–72

The unit on 'The essentials of language' (pages 101–118) explains how to improve grammar, punctuation and spelling.

Test practice on Paper 1 Section C is on page 129; sample students' answers and examiner's comments are on pages 162–180.

> *One Sunday when we were having tea at my Grandparents', the leg fell off the armchair she was sitting on. We thought it was enormously funny, of course, though with the fuss she caused and the anger she displayed towards my Grandad, you'd have thought he had done it on purpose. I wonder if he did?*

Paper 1
Section C Question 4(c)

How well did you do?	**How to improve your level**

Level 4
8–12 marks

Television serials obviously tell stories, and most people love to write stories. In this question, however, students are asked to consider television serials in relation to family life. This is therefore what they must bear in mind, though they will want to describe incidents involving the characters. The 'prompts' (the extra instructions underneath the main question) tell them to think about whether particular programmes are true to life, and to consider particular families.

A level 4 answer may tell only about some incidents concerning characters in the writer's favourite serial, without relating them to family life. The writer will let the sentences run on far too long without searching for exact descriptive words. The writer's use of tenses will also be inconsistent – sometimes writing in the present tense and sometimes in the past tense. The style may be colloquial – that is, writing as you speak. Although the ideas will be organised into correct sentences, punctuation and spelling may be poor because the writer has not checked his or her work.

Typical sentences from a level 4 answer:

> *I love 'Neighbours', and when I was watching last week, Hannah had been having a bad day at school. There was this boy and Hannah and another girl both want him to ask them to go to a dance at the school, so the other girl tells Hannah he has already asked someone else so Hannah will go up to him and have a row about it. This doesn't work because Hannah knows he likes her the most and won't ask anyone else. In the evening, Hannah tells her dad, Philip, all about it and he just smiles in his podgy, cuddly way.*

▷ **If your answer is *level 4*, this is how you might improve on your performance:**

1 Make sure that you really answer the question. This question has two 'prompts' (extra instructions underneath the main question) which tell you to write about family life and realism (being true to life) as they appear in the serials. It is not enough just to tell the story of an incident in a programme which you have seen.

2 Make a plan before you begin writing, so that you organise your writing clearly into paragraphs.

3 You must be consistent with your tenses. If you start with the past tense, which is the most natural tense to use, then stick to it. If you start with the present tense, then stay with that.

4 Do not let your sentences run on until they are too long. Mix long and short sentences, to give a variation. Do not use the word 'so' to connect long phrases, because your sentences will become incorrect.

How well did you do?

Level 5   *14–18 marks*

In a level 5 answer, the style will no longer be colloquial (written as the writer speaks), but the expression will be clear and correct, using exact words. The ideas will be organised into paragraphs and will begin to relate knowledge about the chosen serial to realism (being true to life) and family life. This is partly a discursive question (considering ideas about a subject, rather than just describing it or telling a story) and so there may be no speech used, although it might be more interesting for the reader if it were used. Spelling and punctuation – including full stops, capital letters, commas and apostrophes – will be mostly correct, and handwriting will be clear.

Typical sentences from a level 5 answer:

There are not many complete families in 'Neighbours' now except for the Kennedys. I think this is a shame because when you see parents and teenagers sorting out their problems, it shows you that it can be done in your own family.
There used to be the Robinsons, but now Grandma has died and the others have left the town. In the episode last week, however, Ruth, who has been divorced, was asking her son and daughter whether they would approve if she went to live with Philip and his daughter, Hannah.
'You've got to get a life, Mum,' said Lance. 'Don't worry about us. We can handle it.'

How to improve your level

If your answer is *level 5*, this is how you might improve on your performance:

1 Make sure your writing is well paragraphed, so that the reader can distinguish the different ideas and can follow the stages of your argument.

2 Even in a question like this, it is good to use dialogue (speech) to illustrate points you make, so that the writing seems more lively and natural.

3 Try to choose precise, exact words to express your thoughts and search for the most interesting way of explaining an idea. In our example of level 6 writing (page 23), words such as 'characteristics', 'tensions' and 'conceal' are precise, which add to the quality of the thought and its expression.

4 Make a thorough check of spelling, punctuation and grammar, so that there is no interruption to the flow of your writing.

How well did you do?

Level 6
20–24 marks

This kind of topic is difficult to write about because the writer needs to use ideas to discuss, rather than just telling a story. At this level, the writing will include rather more mature ideas which hold the reader's attention. These ideas will be expressed in some cleverly used words and expressions, which will be included in well-constructed sentences. Any dialogue used will be appropriate to the characters. Punctuation and spelling will be correct in order to help the reader follow the meaning.

Typical sentences from a level 6 answer:

In any family, each member of it has different characteristics and needs which are different from those of the other members.

In 'Neighbours', the tensions created can be seen in the Kennedy family. The mother, Susan, is ambitious in her career as a teacher and has taken a job which takes her away from the family during the week. Carl, the father, who is a doctor, has a receptionist who does not conceal her affection for him. She admires him as a doctor and desires him as a man.

The two children of the family, Billy and Libby, have noticed how often Sarah, the receptionist, visits the house, but neither has yet thought it appropriate to mention the matter to their father.

How to improve your level

▷ **If your answer is *level 6*, this is how you might improve on your performance:**

1 Vary the length of your sentences, so that the reader can easily follow the rhythm of your writing and take in your thoughts and ideas.

2 Search for the most precise, exact words to express your ideas. In our example of level 7 writing (page 24), 'features', 'role models', 'exemplify', 'reciprocated', 'depicted' are precise words which exactly express the ideas the writer wants to communicate.

3 A piece of writing must leave the reader satisfied. At the end, look back over the ideas, or round off the idea you have been leading up to. Leave the reader with a sense of conviction.

How well did you do?

Level 7
26–33 marks

At this level, the writing will be confident and capable in every respect. The words will be well chosen, from a wide range of vocabulary, and will be organised in well-planned paragraphs. There will be variation in sentence structure and a maturity about the ideas which excites the reader. Spelling and punctuation will be almost faultless, and handwriting will be perfectly clear.

Typical sentences from a level 7 answer:

One of the most important features of television serials is that they portray role models which exemplify different points of view. In 'Neighbours', the Bishop and Kennedy families could not show a sharper contrast.

Harold Bishop is a man of clear moral honesty and strength, and would not indulge in any improper activity. By comparison, we are never sure how much temptation Carl Kennedy feels in respect of his attractive receptionist, especially now that his wife is working away. If he was tempted, his feelings would be reciprocated.

The aspect of the role model becomes a factor to be considered when we notice that Harold, who would never err, is depicted as a self-righteous prude, whereas Carl is a handsome, clever, professional man who is well aware of modern trends.

Where to find more help

Collins KS3 English Total Revision has several units on 'Imaginative writing':

Level 4 pages 7–9

Level 5 pages 26–30

Level 6 pages 48–52

Level 7 pages 69–72

The unit on 'The essentials of language' (pages 101–118) explains how to improve grammar, punctuation and spelling.

Test practice on Paper 1 Section C is on page 129; sample students' answers and examiner's comments are on pages 162–180.

ENGLISH TEST PAPER ②

Shakespeare Play

If you have studied ' Henry V', do either task 1 or task 2.

Henry V

Act 1 Scene 2 (line 96 to the end of the scene)

TASK 1

At line 96, King Henry asks Canterbury's advice about whether he should invade France.

Write what advice Canterbury gives to the king, and also write what you think is Canterbury's opinion of Henry as he deals with the French ambassador.

Before you begin to write, you should think about:

* what Henry thinks will happen to England if he goes to France;

* why Canterbury uses the lengthy illustration of the honey bees;

* how Henry reacts to the Dauphin's insult and what Canterbury thinks of this;

* how Canterbury's language varies as he tries to inspire and persuade Henry to attack France.

In the test, the scenes will be given to you in a booklet. To answer the question, refer to your copy of the play.

If you have studied 'Henry V', do either task 1 or task 2.

Henry V

Act 2 Scene 2

TASK 2

In this scene, King Henry deals with three traitors who have plotted with the French to kill him.

Show how in this scene Shakespeare portrays Henry as the complete and perfect king.

Before you begin to write, you should think about:

* how Henry shows that he is in complete control of all the people and the situation;

* the comparison between Henry's mercy towards the prisoner in lines 40-43 and his justice towards Cambridge, Scroop and Gray;

* how Henry is a man of quick and decisive action;

* how Henry's language varies as the situations change.

In the test, the scenes will be given to you in a booklet. To answer the question, refer to your copy of the play.

If you have studied 'Macbeth', do either task 3 or task 4.

Macbeth

Act 2 Scenes 1 and 2

TASK 3

If you were directing a performance of this scene, what would you tell the actors performing the parts of Macbeth and Lady Macbeth in order to make the events as dramatic as possible?

Before you begin to write, you should think about:

* Macbeth's and Lady Macbeth's states of mind, both before and after the murder;

* how Macbeth reacts to the ghostly dagger;

* how Lady Macbeth manages Macbeth after the murder.

In the test, the scenes will be given to you in a booklet. To answer the question, refer to your copy of the play.

If you have studied 'Macbeth', do either task 3 or task 4.

Macbeth

Act 4 Scene 1

TASK 4

In this scene, Macbeth consults the witches about his future.

Explain how the witches lead Macbeth to his downfall.

Before you begin to write, you should think about:

* the tricks contained in the predictions;

* the way in which Macbeth is persuaded to act on impulse and instinct;

* the references to evil in the scene.

In the test, the scenes will be given to you in a booklet. To answer the question, refer to your copy of the play.

If you have studied 'Twelfth Night', do either task 5 or task 6.

Twelfth Night

Act 3 Scene 4 (lines 1 to 167)

TASK 5

This scene deals with two letters: the one Malvolio has previously found in the garden and its effects, and the one Sir Andrew writes to Cesario.

Imagine you are Maria, commenting on the fun in this scene.

Before you begin to write, you should think about:

* your part in the trick;

* how Malvolio made a fool of himself and the consequences;

* the different ways in which Sir Andrew was made to look ridiculous;

* the part played by Sir Toby.

You could begin, 'I have never laughed so much in one afternoon...'

In the test, the scenes will be given to you in a booklet. To answer the question, refer to your copy of the play.

If you have studied 'Twelfth Night', do either task 5 or task 6.

Twelfth Night

Act 1 Scene 5 (line 81 to the end)

TASK 6

In this scene, Olivia meets Viola, who is disguised as a young man, Cesario. Viola has been sent to Olivia by Orsino.

Write about the feelings that Olivia has in this scene towards the people who speak with her: Malvolio, Sir Toby, and especially Viola.

Before you begin to write, you should think about:

* the characters of Malvolio and Sir Toby;

* why Olivia at first refuses to see Viola;

* why Olivia talks for some time with Viola and asks her to return.

In the test, the scenes will be given to you in a booklet. To answer the question, refer to your copy of the play.

HOW TO MARK YOUR ANSWER

The different types of questions

The Shakespeare questions that are set in the test are of three types.

First, there is the 'critical discussion' question that asks you to show your knowledge by writing about what happens in any one scene – descriptions or explanations of plot, character, meaning or language.

Second, there is the 'empathetic' question where you imagine you are one of the characters and show your knowledge of plot, character and meaning by writing as if you are that person.

Third, you may be asked to imagine you are directing what happens on the stage in a scene. You are expected to show your knowledge of plot, character and meaning by writing what you would tell the actors to do.

The first of these types of questions – the 'critical discussion' question – is the one that is most frequently set.

How well did you do?

Examiners give *two types of marks* for answers to questions on Shakespeare texts. For **Understanding** they mark answers according to these criteria:

1 *Plot* – you must know what happens in each scene.

2 *Character* – each person in the play has different characteristics, which you must know and understand.

3 *Meaning* – this refers to the ideas in the play. Sometimes it is called the theme.

4 *Language* – Shakespeare's poetry is very rich in meaning and colour. The style of language changes from character to character. You must try to appreciate this.

5 *Relevance* – you must make sure that what you write exactly answers the question.

Examiners also award marks for **Writing Skills** in answers to Shakespeare questions. These marks are given according to the same criteria that are used for writing in Paper 1 Section C:

1 *What you write.* The number and quality of ideas.

2 *Structure.* The quality of the beginning and ending of your answers will be assessed. Examiners will also be looking for varied sentence structure and appropriate paragraphing.

3 *Expression.* Examiners will assess your style of writing. This means they will look at how exact and appropriate your choice of words and phrases is. They will look at how you arrange your words and phrases.

4 *Accuracy.* Examiners will assess how accurate your spelling, punctuation and grammar are, and how legible your handwriting is.

In order to work out what level you would be awarded for the answer you have written, read the assessment guidance given for each level, both for understanding and written expression. Then read the type of sentences that would occur in answers at each level. You will not have written exactly the same sentences, but you should be able to tell whether the quality of your writing is the same. See if you can match your answer to a level. If you are unsure, ask someone you can trust – a relative or friend – to help you.

How to improve your level

Once you have decided what level your answer would probably be given, look at the column headed 'How to improve your level' which is alongside. This suggests what you need to do to improve your answer so that you can do better next time, and achieve a higher level.

Where to find more help

This section includes detailed references to *Collins KS3 English Total Revision*. Whichever level you are working at, this book will help you to develop the skills you need to answer questions on your Shakespeare play.

Henry V
Task 1

How well did you do?

Level 4

Understanding   *6–8 marks*

A level 4 answer will deal only with the first and third prompts. (The prompts are the points with a star underneath the main question – they are there to guide you). This is because they deal with what happens. Henry is worried about the Scots invading from the north when he is away in France, but Canterbury strongly advises him that England can defend itself and live happily. A level 4 answer will show understanding that Henry is annoyed by the tennis balls, but will not discuss the way he controls his anger.

Writing Skills   *4–6 marks*

Canterbury's advice to go to France, and Henry's anger about the tennis balls will be clearly stated. The writing will be mostly in correct sentences, with punctuation and full stops accurately used. There will be a narrow range of vocabulary and the simple words will usually be spelled correctly. Handwriting will be clear and readable.

Typical remarks in a level 4 answer:

> *Canterbury is all for Henry going to war with France, and he tells him to remember his ancestors and to go and attack them. He tells Henry not to bother about the Scots because, just like they have done before, the English people will deal with them, and will be safe while Henry is away.*
> *Henry calls in the French ambassador to say what the Dauphin thinks and the Dauphin has sent a message that Henry cannot have a claim to any part of France. He says the Dauphin has sent some treasure, but when they open it up it is tennis balls. Henry is really annoyed at this and sends a message that this is no joke. He will go to France and kill many, many Frenchmen and get his kingdom.*

How to improve your level

▷ **If your answer is *level 4*, this is how you might improve on your performance:**

1 Follow **all** the prompts, not just the easiest ones: if you only use half the prompts, you start with a maximum of half marks. You are, therefore, only going to gain only a small proportion of the total marks available.

2 Do not just state the simple facts of the scene, but give more detail from the text about the characters' feelings and motives.

3 Use quotations from the text, as well as detailed reference, in your answer. Use inverted commas, and write out quotations in lines of poetry, as in the text. Check each sentence you write, trying to get a sense of the rhythm, so that the full stops and other punctuation marks are in the right places.

How well did you do?

Level 5

Understanding   *10–12 marks*

At level 5, the answer will just be a straightforward commentary. That is, it states what happens in the scene, without any thoughtful comments about why characters say what they do, what their motives are, and what effect they want to produce on others. Some quotations will be used, and there will be enough detail to make an answer of reasonable length.

Writing Skills   *7–9 marks*

Paragraphs will be well-organised and there will be more precision in the choice of words and phrases to express ideas. Spelling of all the simple words, and most of the complex words, will be accurate. All punctuation marks will be used correctly. Handwriting will be clear and well-formed.

Typical remarks in a level 5 answer:

Canterbury really encourages King Henry to invade France, and he refers to the Bible and Henry's ancestors to give him good reason to attack. Ely and Exeter speak in the same tone, before Canterbury joins in the persuasion again, promising that the church will raise a lot of money to help his army. Henry is worried about the Scots invading while he is out of the country, but Canterbury reassures him that this has happened, and the English who have been left at home have easily dealt with the warlike Scots.
He goes on to say that in a country, every person has their job to do, their role to play. Just as in a beehive there are many different types of bee, and each has its own function, so, in a country, some people go abroad to fight, while others stay at home and organise things for the good of everyone. This convinced Henry, and he became

How well did you do?

determined to overcome the French. First, he received the French ambassador, who denied that Henry had any legal claim to France, and he said that the Dauphin thought that he must be as mad as he was when he was young. He then insulted Henry by saying that he had sent him a ton of treasure, and this turned out to be tennis balls.
Here, all those in court expected Henry to explode with rage, but he was quite calm and collected as he promised to hit the balls back with such force that they would become gun-stones. Canterbury would have admired the strength and determination of Henry's reply to the Dauphin:

> *'And tell the Dauphin*
> *His jest will savour but of shallow wit*
> *When thousands weep more than did laugh at it.'*

Canterbury would have been happy that Henry is doing what he wanted.

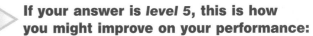

How to improve your level

▷ **If your answer is *level 5*, this is how you might improve on your performance:**

1 Use more quotations, but build them into your answer: make them short, but part of the sentence, or part of the thought, not just added on to the end, as is the one in the level 5 answer.

2 Do not just tell the story, but try to get beneath the surface of how and why Canterbury gives the advice he does, and write as much as you can about his opinions.

3 Work hard on your choice of words and phrases, and check the accuracy of your spelling and punctuation.

How well did you do?

Level 6

Understanding   *14–16 marks*

A level 6 answer looks more thoughtfully at the question. Canterbury is seen as a representative of the church, which has special reasons for wanting Henry to go to war with France. These reasons are why Canterbury looks critically at Henry's character and at how he behaves. He very much likes what he sees.

Writing Skills   *10–12 marks*

Clear expression will be helped by well-organised paragraphing and well-structured sentences. The words and phrases will be very precisely chosen. Punctuation will be used correctly and the spelling, even of complex words, will be good. Handwriting will be regular and easy to read.

Typical remarks in a level 6 answer:

Canterbury is so enthusiastic about persuading Henry to go to war in order to claim the throne of France because the church is afraid that he will take much of its wealth away. There was already a law that the king could do this, but Canterbury knows that if the king is occupied in France, he will not have time for such designs. Therefore, having quoted the Bible in support of his claim, Canterbury urges Henry to:
'Stand for your own, unwind your bloody flag, Look back into your mighty ancestors'
and capture his kingdom by force. He even promises Henry 'a mighty sum' of money from the church, because the war is in the church's interest. Ely, Exeter and Westmoreland all support this advice. Henry's main worry is invasion by the Scots when the English army is away, but Canterbury reassures him about this and then describes a kingdom in which each member has his own function which

How well did you do?

contributes to the common well-being, so that
'a thousand actions, once afoot End in one purpose, and be all well borne Without defeat.'
This makes up Henry's mind, but when he calls in the French ambassador, he is insulted by being called a youth and being presented with tennis balls instead of treasure. Canterbury is then full of admiration as he watches Henry reply in a way which is at first calm and firm, but then becomes threatening and belligerent. He must have thought he had done his job of persuasion well, because there was no trace of doubt or hesitation in Henry.

How to improve your level

▷ **If your answer is *level 6*, this is how you might improve on your performance:**

1 Develop further the motives behind Canterbury's advice and trace his thoughts about the situation in England and how Henry reacts to the Dauphin's insult.

2 The level 6 answer given here deals adequately with the first three prompts. Try to say something about the quality of the language as well as building quotations into the thought content of your answer.

3 You need to aim for the best possible clarity and accuracy in punctuation and sentence structure. Check your spelling so that you avoid any errors and make sure your handwriting is as well-formed and clear as possible. Always search for the best possible words and phrases to express your ideas.

Level 7

Understanding   *18–22 marks*

At level 7, the answer will explore the text carefully. It will discuss not only what Canterbury advises, but **why** he, and therefore the church, are so keen to urge Henry to invade France. It will show the difference between Canterbury's belligerent and violent language at the beginning, the measured and calm description of a united kingdom in the middle of the scene, and the increasing tempo of Henry's speech at the end. Canterbury's motives, thoughts and opinions will be made relevant to the question throughout the answer, and will link both halves of the question.

Writing Skills   *13–16 marks*

The writing will be fluent, confident and well-organised into paragraphs. The choice of vocabulary and the sentence structure will give precise and clear expression of the writer's ideas. Sentences will be accurately formed and punctuated and will show a variation in their structures. The spelling of simple and complex words will be accurate, and handwriting will be clear and regular.

Typical remarks in a level 7 answer:

The passion and conviction with which Canterbury urges Henry to invade France and so claim his throne, can be seen by the menacing and belligerent tone he adopts:
'Stand for your own, unwind your bloody flag,
Look back into your mighty ancestors...
...invoke his warlike spirit.'
After support from Ely, Exeter and Westmoreland, he still encourages him:
'With blood and sword and fire to win your right.'
To Canterbury, Henry's fears of invasion by the Scots when the English army is away show a danger that Henry might waver in his resolve to go to war, and so he maintains his confidence and force:

'She hath been then more feared than harmed, my liege.'
Because Westmoreland and Exeter keep Henry's fears alive, Canterbury changes to a more calm and measured and rational manner of persuasion. Just like a beehive, he argues, a kingdom is a pattern of interdependent people and their functions:
'So many a thousand actions, once afoot,
End in one purpose, and be all well borne Without defeat. Therefore to France, my liege.'
Once Henry has decided to subjugate France 'by God's help', Canterbury becomes a spectator, as the king receives the French ambassador and suffers the insult of the Dauphin's 'tun of treasure' which turns out to be tennis balls. There is, however, no doubt about how high in his esteem Henry rises as he reacts to the Dauphin's message. There is no impulsive anger.
But there is a menacing swell of threat and defiance:
'I will dazzle all the eyes of France,
Yea, strike the Dauphin blind to look on us.'
Canterbury must have been happy that the king is doing exactly what he wanted.

Where to find more help

Collins KS3 English Total Revision has a whole chapter on 'Reading and Writing about Shakespeare'. This chapter is suitable for you to read no matter which Shakespeare play you are studying or which level you are working at. It shows you how to improve your reading and writing skills and so move your Test answer to a higher level.

Chapter 21 of *Collins KS3 English Total Revision* gives you detailed guidance on 'Test Techniques Paper 2' which you need to develop in order to tackle the Shakespeare play successfully.

Two further Test practice tasks on 'Henry V' can be found in Chapter 23 of *Collins KS3 English Total Revision*, with help and guidance in Chapter 27.

Henry V
Task 2

Level 4

Understanding   *6–8 marks*

A level 4 answer will describe the events of the scene without much comment on the manner in which Henry deals with them. It will deal with Henry's previous knowledge of the traitors' crimes, and the fact that Henry released the prisoner, but will not discuss Henry's control of the situation. There will be no distinction between the way he treats each of the traitors, and no contrast shown between his dealing with the men and his preparations to sail to France.

Writing Skills   *4–6 marks*

The ideas will be arranged in such a way that the reader can easily follow what the writer means. The ideas will be straightforward and the expression will be simple in terms of the words and phrases used and the way the sentences are constructed. There will probably be no paragraphing. Full stops and other punctuation marks will be mostly correct. Simple words will be spelled correctly, and handwriting will be reasonably clear.

Typical remarks in a level 4 answer:

Henry must be in complete control of things because Bedford tells the audience that he knows what the traitors have done before they set sail for France from Southampton. The three traitors, Cambridge, Scroop and Gray, flatter the king before they know that they have been found out, and they also say that he should not show any mercy to the prisoner who has insulted him. When Henry lets them know that their treason has been discovered, all three beg for mercy in a quite sickening way. The king then makes a long speech in which he tells them off for their treachery and says that, however loudly they cry out for pardon, they will have to die for their crimes according to the law. Then he makes preparations to put to sea.

▷ **If your answer is *level 4*, this is how you might improve on your performance:**

1 Do not be satisfied with describing only an outline of the events which occur in the scene. By looking more closely at the text, **make inferences** about what each event tells the audience about the motives and thoughts of the characters, especially those of Henry. For instance, compare the way that Cambridge, Scroop and Gray say that mercy should not be shown to the prisoner, but then they beg for pardon for themselves.

2 Use quotation and more detailed reference to the text. These will show that you understand and know about the play in detail and not just the general drift of it. When you quote, write out the text in lines of poetry.

3 Check your spelling and punctuation, including the full stops, to make sure that they are correct so that the reader can clearly understand your meaning. Try to widen your vocabulary and vary the length of your sentences. Write in paragraphs, as this, more than anything else, is a sign of a well-organised answer.

How well did you do?

Level 5

Understanding   *10–12 marks*

A level 5 answer will consist of an account of the scene with some quotations to illustrate the comments that are being made. There may be a little comment on what each event shows in terms of character, but this will be very limited. Only about half of the guidelines given in the prompts for the question will be followed.

Writing Skills   *7–9 marks*

The ideas will be clearly organised into paragraphs. The sentences will have a reasonably varied length and structure, and vocabulary will be chosen effectively. Full stops, capital letters, commas, apostrophes and quotation marks will be used accurately. The spelling will be good, though there may be errors in harder words, and handwriting will be clear.

Typical remarks in a level 5 answer:

Henry showed his control over people and events as he and his army were about to embark for France, because the Dukes of Bedford and Exeter, as well as the Earl of Westmoreland, tell the audience that he intends to arrest the traitors at any moment. He does not do this immediately, but discusses the prospect of the invasion with them and they flatter his popularity and mention the good spirits of his army.

   When Henry tells Exeter to set free the prisoner who was drunk and insulted him, then Scroop, Cambridge and Gray say that he should have no mercy:

'Let him be punished, sovereign, lest example Breed by his sufferance more of such a kind.'

   Just after that, though, Henry gives the three men their letters of commission for France, and it turns out that they are their indictments and warrants for arrest for treason. Once they realised that the game was up and begged for mercy, Henry really

How well did you do?

turned on them, saying they had not wanted mercy for the prisoner, and called them 'English monsters'. He is strongest in his condemnation of Scroop, calling him a 'cruel, Ingrateful savage and inhuman creature', and finally saying,

'For this revolt of thine, methinks, is like Another fall of man.'

   As soon as he has pronounced their death sentences, Henry does not linger, but immediately makes practical arrangements to embark for France.

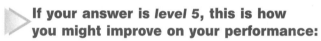

How to improve your level

▷ **If your answer is *level 5*, this is how you might improve on your performance:**

1 Most of the level 5 answer given here is straightforward narrative: that is, it tells the story of the scene without any comment on the motives and feelings of the characters or on the general meaning of the play. You need to comment on **motivation**, **feeling** and **theme** to move beyond level 5.

2 Explore the text **in more detail**, and each time Henry takes action or makes a decisive comment, point this out and say how it must have seemed to those present, either inspiring respect or arousing fear.

3 Check that your sentences are properly constructed and that there is some variation in their length. Check also that your punctuation - capital letters, full stops, commas, apostrophes and quotation marks - are correct. Make sure that your spelling, even of the more difficult words, is accurate and that your handwriting is clear.

How well did you do?

Level 6

Understanding   14–16 marks

At level 6, an answer will not only give an account of all the important events and speeches in a scene, but will also make comments on their **significance**. That is, the writer will mention the motives and feelings of characters and show what effect each speech and action has on others. The answer will include some statements about the meaning of these events, speeches and feelings as far as the whole play is concerned. All this will be well supported by textual reference and quotation.

Writing Skills   10–12 marks

The expression will be clear, well-organised in sentences and paragraphs, and written in an appropriate style. All aspects of punctuation will be correct, and the vocabulary and phrases will be chosen with as much precision as possible. Spelling, even of more difficult words, will be correct. Handwriting will be well-formed and clear.

Typical remarks in a level 6 answer:

Henry's control over the characters and events in this scene is shown right at the beginning when there is an air of expectation as the king and the English army are about to embark to go and invade France. The Duke of Bedford tells the audience that Henry is well aware of the way in which the three traitors have tried to betray him.

However, when he comes in, he conceals this by talking about the prospects for the voyage and the invasion. He also accepts in a commanding way the flattery which Scroop, Cambridge and Gray heap upon him.

It is with deliberate calculation and perfect timing that Henry orders Exeter to release the prisoner who, the day before, insulted the king while he was drunk. Cambridge, Scroop and Gray protest at this,

How well did you do?

saying that if this man is excused, it might encourage others to do the same. Henry, however, shows understanding, compassion and tolerance:

'If little faults, proceeding on distemper,
Shall not be wink'd at, how shall we stretch our eye
When capital crimes, chew'd, swallowed and digested, Appear before us?'

The calculation with which he introduced this apparently trivial matter, and the effectiveness of his timing are shown when he gives the three nobles their letters of commission for France, and they prove to be warrants for their arrest on charges of high treason.

After this, the swift decisiveness of the death sentence he passes on them is seen by all present as perfectly just, and Henry turns to make practical arrangements for embarkation for France.

How to improve your level

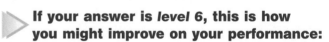

If your answer is *level 6*, this is how you might improve on your performance:

1 The motives and feelings of characters and the general significance of their actions have been included in the level 6 answer given here. Try to add further to these, illustrating them with appropriate quotations which are a natural part of the argument.

2 As well as dealing with the first three prompts in your answer in a balanced way, explore the way the language varies in the different situations, and relate this to the events and characters, especially to Henry.

3 Aim for absolute clarity in punctuation and sentence structure. Check spelling so that you avoid any errors, and make your handwriting as regular and clear as possible. Always search for the best possible words or phrases to express your ideas.

How well did you do?

Level 7

Understanding   *18–22 marks*

A level 7 answer will make everything relevant to the question and therefore relate all the events and characters' reactions to Henry's role: his awareness of the conspiracy, and the calm, calculated and well-timed way that he deals with it; the fact that he can be magnanimous and compassionate to the relatively trivial transgression of the prisoner; the fact that he organises practical matters quickly and efficiently; his meting out of severe justice to the traitors. All these are the right and necessary qualities for a king leading his nation into war, and all these are shown in the scene.

Writing Skills   *13–16 marks*

The writing will be well-organised in paragraphs, each of which will deal with an aspect of Henry's character as shown in each event of the scene. The sentences will be accurately formed and structured. Punctuation will be used accurately to clarify meaning and the spelling of simple and complex words will be good. Words and phrases will be precisely chosen and there will be an avoidance of any colloquial diction. Handwriting will be well-formed and easy to read.

Typical remarks in a level 7 answer:

The fact that the Duke of Bedford tells the audience right at the beginning of the scene that Henry is well aware of the conspiracy against him, shows that he is well in control of events and characters. He appears not to worry about it when he first enters, chatting amiably with the three traitors, Cambridge, Scroop and Gray, and seeming more concerned to get his army conveyed to France so that they can get about their business.

He even allows them to condemn themselves by suggesting that Henry should show no mercy to the prisoner who insulted Henry while he was drunk. Henry, however, prefers to be understanding and forgiving towards

Where to find more help

'little faults, proceeding on distemper'. When he actually deals with the traitors, he does it deftly by delivering their arrest warrants when they think they are letters of commission for France. Because he knows very clearly what he must do as king and ruler, Henry will not listen to their pathetic, self-interested pleas for mercy. He makes it clear that it is not a matter of personal revenge, but of state security:

> *'Touching our person seek we no revenge,*
> *But we our kingdom's safety must so tender,*
> *Whose ruin you have sought, that to her laws*
>   *We do deliver you.'*

Henry does, though, show a human aspect by being especially affected by the treachery of his closest confidant, Scroop. He directs a lengthy tirade of accusation against Scroop, consisting not only of measured insults ('Ingrateful, savage and inhuman creature'), but also a series of rhetorical questions to which he supplies the incriminating answers so that his crimes are seen as having the widest historical significance:
>   *'Another fall of man'.*

Where to find more help

Collins KS3 English Total Revision has a whole chapter on 'Reading and Writing about Shakespeare'. This chapter is suitable for you to read no matter which Shakespeare play you are studying or which level you are working at. It shows you how to improve your reading and writing skills and so move your Test answer to a higher level.

Chapter 21 of *Collins KS3 English Total Revision* gives you detailed guidance on 'Test Techniques Paper 2' which you need to develop in order to tackle the Shakespeare play successfully.

Two further Test practice tasks on 'Henry V' can be found in Chapter 23 of *Collins KS3 English Total Revision*, with help and guidance in Chapter 27.

Macbeth
Task 3

How well did you do?	How to improve your level

Level 4

Understanding   6–8 marks

A level 4 answer will concentrate on a general comparison between Macbeth and Lady Macbeth, telling her to be in charge of the situation, with Macbeth the reluctant partner. It may talk about how Macbeth can make the dagger appear realistic, or other staging ideas. It will discuss what happens in the scenes rather than the **effects of the speeches**.

Writing Skills   4–6 marks

Ideas will be clearly expressed with some suitable organisation, such as paragraphing or sub-headings. There will be an attempt to sound like a director. Punctuation of sentences will be mostly accurate and most common words will be spelt correctly. Handwriting will be mostly clear.

Typical remarks in a level 4 answer:

Macbeth, when you see the dagger you must look shocked. After a bit you think it is showing you the way, so you are not so scared. When the bell rings it makes you jump, so I want to see a reaction.

Lady Macbeth, before the murder you are lively because you have been drinking, but when the owl shrieks you are not quite so brave. When Macbeth comes in you are still tense and you think he has not done the murder.

After the murder you are feeling the stress, Macbeth, because the guards were having nightmares and you wanted them to be quiet, so you get really wound up about not being able to say 'amen'.

Lady Macbeth, you must sort him out. If he won't pull himself together he might spoil things. You have to push him to make him wash his hands and really shout at him.

▷ **If your answer is *level 4*, this is how you might improve on your performance:**

1 Try to show more detailed understanding of the ways in which the characters react to each other. Imagine how annoyed Lady Macbeth is getting because Macbeth changes his mind, and how she can show this on stage.

2 Remember that Macbeth commits an enormous crime and it is having a big effect on the way he behaves. Think about which words in his speeches best show his emotions.

3 Refer to what the characters say as much as you can in your answer. Check that you have expressed yourself clearly and you have the punctuation marks in the correct places. Check your spellings.

How well did you do?

Level 5

Understanding   *10–12 marks*

A level 5 answer will give a commentary on the different reactions of Macbeth and Lady Macbeth to the situation. Macbeth may be told to look anxious and confused when he is speaking particular lines; Lady Macbeth may be told to shout at him or to get hold of him when she is forcing him to act in a particular way. The answer will recognise that some parts of the scenes are more dramatic than others. There will be some references to the text.

Writing Skills   *7–9 marks*

The writing will be organised into paragraphs. Expression will show some careful choices of words to give advice. There will be a range of punctuation marks used, usually accurately. Spelling will be mostly accurate, even in longer words. Handwriting will usually be clear.

Typical remarks in a level 5 answer:

When you are making your long dagger speech, Macbeth, pace up and down and act in an anxious way. When you say 'Come, let me clutch thee', try several times to grab hold of the dagger and be sometimes quiet and sometimes really loud because you are talking to yourself.

Lady Macbeth, you must be much more confident because you are more ruthless than your husband. When you first come in you are pleased with yourself because you have got the guards drunk and have had a drink yourself. When the owl hoots you jump at first but quickly realise it is just a normal night noise. Macbeth comes in and I want you to show a bit of panic when you say:

'Alack, I am afraid they have awaked and 'tis not done'.

You can also look a bit sad when you say Duncan looked like your father.

How well did you do?

After the murder there is more difference between the way you both behave. Macbeth must be confused and drifting about the stage but Lady Macbeth must take charge and steer him towards where she wants him to go.

How to improve your level

▷ **If your answer is *level 5*, this is how you might improve on your performance:**

1   Make sure that you stick as closely to the events in the scenes as you can, and pick out the most distinctive contrasts between the ways in which the characters behave. Try to support what you say by referring directly to the text.

2   Point out that the dagger scene is very dramatic because it may be a supernatural link with the witches; the second scene is also high drama because Duncan's murder is the first really bad deed Macbeth has committed.

3   When you have checked that your writing is as clear and accurate as you can make it, try to choose interesting and varied vocabulary to make your explanations more precise.

How well did you do?

Level 6

Understanding   *14–16 marks*

A level 6 answer will tackle in some detail the ways in which the characters speak to the audience and to each other to create levels of tension. The answer will be focused and will explore the text whilst suggesting interpretations. The main themes of the play will be acknowledged. There will be some examination of the relative evil evident in the characters at this point in the action.

Writing Skills   *10–12 marks*

Explanations will be clear and appropriately organised into paragraphs. Expression, spelling and punctuation will be good. There will be a variety of different sentence types used to add more interest for the reader.

Typical remarks in a level 6 answer:

After you have got rid of Banquo by fobbing him off, Macbeth, you prepare yourself mentally for the murder. This is when the dagger appears. You need to show to the audience that you are struggling to interpret the meaning of the dagger, whether it is there to prick your conscience or whether it is to give you a lead what to do next. Remember you are talking to the audience here. When you get to the part of the speech beginning, 'Now o'er the one half world', the mood should be much darker and the words pronounced more viciously.

Lady Macbeth, although you must appear jumpy when the owl hoots, you are excited about what is happening. Later you get frustrated with your husband when he loses control, letting his conscience get the better of him, ranting about sleep, rather than acting quickly to cover up the crime. You must appear very decisive and forceful here.

How to improve your level

If your answer is *level* 6, this is how you might improve on your performance:

1   Emphasise the different moods and emotions which Macbeth goes through during these scenes, perhaps even referring to the earlier meeting with the witches, where his reaction showed that murdering the king had already crossed his mind before.

2   Use the scene following the murder to emphasise the contrast between the actions of Macbeth and his wife. The handwashing section is a good example: Macbeth thinks there is not enough water in the world to wash away Duncan's blood, whereas Lady Macbeth says, 'A little water clears us of this deed.' This might be developed by a reference to the later sleepwalking scene, in which she says, 'Will these hands ne'er be clean?'

3   Select your words really carefully, trying to avoid repeating yourself. You can add realism to the voice of the director by introducing some theatrical terms, such as 'soliloquy', 'front of stage', 'gesture', 'articulate your words slowly/quickly'.

How well did you do?

Level 7

Understanding   *18–22 marks*

A level 7 answer will give very clear and positive direction to the actors. It will be the voice of authority and will consider the shades of meaning in the text as well as overall impressions. It will show the changing reactions of Macbeth and his wife at the different stages of the scenes. The advice given will be detailed and concentrate on the effects of the language. Comments will be justified by careful reference to the text.

Writing Skills   *13–16 marks*

The writing will be confident, organised and in the appropriate tone for giving advice in a professional way. The careful choice of vocabulary and use of different sentence types will add to the clarity of the piece.

Typical remarks in a level 7 answer:

Macbeth, when delivering your soliloquy, make use of gesture to the audience to establish your relationship with them. The turmoil in your mind manifests itself by the vision of the dagger – be convincing in your visualisation of the weapon; show horror at the 'fatal vision' and 'gouts of blood'. Grope for the ghostly dagger frantically, coming to front of stage and showing the audience the terror in your eyes. In the second half of the speech, when you talk of the powers of darkness, reduce your voice to a fearful whisper to convey that you are afraid to speak of these things out loud.

When your husband has done the deed, Lady Macbeth, you are the dominant presence on the stage; hound him to find out the details of the murder, spit the lines into his face when you are scorning him; physically push him around the stage when you are wanting him to wash away the evidence and get to bed.

Where to find more help

Collins KS3 English Total Revision has a whole chapter on 'Reading and Writing about Shakespeare'. This chapter is suitable for you to read no matter which Shakespeare play you are studying or which level you are working at. It shows you how to improve your reading and writing skills and so move your Test answer to a higher level.

Chapter 21 of *Collins KS3 English Total Revision* gives you detailed guidance on 'Test Techniques Paper 2' which you need to develop in order to tackle the Shakespeare play successfully.

Two further Test practice tasks on 'Macbeth' can be found in Chapter 23 of *Collins KS3 English Total Revision*, with help and guidance in Chapter 28.

Macbeth
Task 4

How well did you do?	How to improve your level

Level 4

Understanding   *6–8 marks*

A level 4 answer will contain some comments about how Macbeth demands to know his future and most of the answer will tell about the apparitions and what they say. There will be a little explanation of how Macbeth misinterprets the predictions. There may be some quotations from the scene but they may not add to what has already been said.

Writing Skills   *4–6 marks*

The ideas will be clearly expressed and sentences will be organised into paragraphs with punctuation mostly sound. Spelling will be generally accurate and the handwriting mostly clear.

Typical remarks in a level 4 answer:

The witches were a very bad influence on Macbeth. He went to see them because things weren't going right even after he had killed Duncan and Banquo. The witches really tricked him because the first cauldron figure said he'd better watch out for Macduff, 'Beware Macduff, beware the Thane of Fife' but then the second one said that no man of woman born could beat him. The third one said that he would not be defeated till Birnam Wood came up Dunsinane Hill, which was totally unlikely. Macbeth thought that he had been right to be suspicious of Macduff and that from now on when he thought of something, he would do it without waiting. The witches are quite evil and so is Macbeth now because he doesn't have any second thoughts about killing people.

If your answer is *level 4*, this is how you might improve on your performance:

1 Do not just tell the story. Try to explain the two different interpretations of each apparition's message.

2 You need to give the example of the impulsive decision which he makes to slaughter the whole of Macduff's household.

3 For the third prompt, you need to pick out some of the evil mentions and ingredients of the witches and say how Macbeth is getting more like the weird sisters.

How well did you do?

Level 5

Understanding   *10–12 marks*

A level 5 answer will give a straightforward commentary, providing an overview of the scene. It will show understanding of Macbeth's anxiety to know his future and will explain what the apparitions' riddles mean. The answer will mention what the characters say, or give direct quotations.

Writing Skills   *7–9 marks*

The writing will be clearly organised into paragraphs. The explanations will be expressed using different lengths of sentences to develop some of the ideas. Punctuation such as commas, apostrophes and speech marks will be used accurately. The spelling of most words will be correct and the handwriting will be clear.

Typical remarks in a level 5 answer:

Macbeth goes to see the witches because he is uncertain about his future. They know he is coming and they prepare a spell with all sorts of disgusting ingredients which the audience at that time would find really evil.

Macbeth starts off being rude to the witches and calls them 'midnight hags'. He is determined to know what might happen and orders them to tell him. They ask whether he wants to hear it from them or their masters and straightaway he chooses the masters.

The first vision is an armed head which tells him to 'beware Macduff' and Macbeth is pleased with himself because he already suspected Macduff. The second vision is a bloody child which says 'none of woman born Shall harm Macbeth'. So Macbeth thinks there was no point to the first warning but he decides to do something about it anyway. The third vision is a child crowned with a tree in his hand who tells him, 'Macbeth

How well did you do?

shall never vanquished be until Great Birnam Wood to high Dunsinane Hill Shall come against him'. Macbeth thinks that can never happen.

The truth is that Macduff was born by caesarean and eventually kills Macbeth and the soldiers cut down branches of the wood for camouflage, so they all come true.

How to improve your level

▷ **If your answer is *level 5*, this is how you might improve on your performance:**

1 Make sure you take care to answer each of the prompts fully, rather than with just a passing statement. Do not be too carried away giving explanations of what the predictions mean.

2 When you use quotations, make sure your own words show that you know what they mean.

3 Construct your sentences carefully; do not ramble.

How well did you do?

Level 6

Understanding   *14–16 marks*

A level 6 answer will show a deeper understanding of how Macbeth is becoming more and more evil. The answer will explore the text: there will be detailed comments on some parts of the scene, with suitable supporting references and quotations.

Writing Skills   *10–12 marks*

The writing will be clearly organised in paragraphs. The range of different sentence types used will give a fluent explanation. Vocabulary will be varied and the spelling of words will be mostly accurate. It will be in well-presented handwriting.

Typical remarks in a level 6 answer:

When Macbeth went to see the witches he was already in quite a reckless state of mind and determined to know what was in store for him. It was therefore obvious that when the witches' guiding spirits spoke to him, he would believe and act on everything that they told him. Unfortunately for Macbeth, the statements they gave him were not what they seemed.

The first apparition, a soldier's head, represented Macduff, whom Macbeth suspected to be his enemy. He was told Macduff was dangerous, so the fact that the witches reinforced his own opinion made him more willing to believe the rest. The second apparition was a baby covered in blood, and represented Macduff being born by caesarean section, but when Macbeth was told no-one 'of woman born' would be able to harm him, he took it to mean that no-one at all would be able to kill him, not even Macduff. The third apparition, a child with a crown on his head and a branch in his hand, represented the young Prince Malcolm and told Macbeth he would never be defeated until Birnam Wood climbed up Dunsinane

How well did you do?

Hill. At this point Macbeth, not seeing beneath the obvious, thought he would be safe: 'our high-placed Macbeth Shall live the lease of nature'. But his confidence takes a blow when he asks about Banquo's descendants ruling Scotland and he is shown a long line of kings, all looking just like his former fellow soldier.

This last experience made him even more desperate and bloodthirsty. He believed in the deceitful statements of the witches, not realising that they all had a twist to them. When he saw the last vision it made him so angry that he decided he would take his revenge by acting on every aggressive thought which came into his head.

How to improve your level

▷ **If your answer is *level 6*, this is how you might improve on your performance:**

1 You might extend your explanation of the witches' double-dealing by explaining what the outcome of Macbeth's confusion actually was.

2 You need to target particular words and phrases in the scene which show deceit, recklessness and evil – in order to cover all the prompts comprehensively.

3 Be very careful about your choice of words and phrases in your explanations and check spellings and punctuation, especially in long sentences.

How well did you do?

Level 7

Understanding   *18–22 marks*
A level 7 answer will be a full one which shows great familiarity with the play. It will address the question clearly, tracing the deterioration in Macbeth's control over his actions. The significant phrases from the scene are identified, with helpful commentary.

Writing Skills   *13–16 marks*
The writing will be confident and well-organised into paragraphs, with stylish and varied sentence structures. Vocabulary will be effective and punctuation helpful. Spelling, even of the more difficult words, will be correct.

Typical remarks in a level 7 answer:

'A deed without a name' is how the witches describe their spell when Macbeth meets them in this scene. This gives a clue as to the evil inherent in their actions. This is reinforced by the list of vile ingredients which have been put into the cauldron.

Although Macbeth's previous meeting with the witches had led him from being a good and loyal subject to a ruthless murderer, he has now degenerated so far that he actively seeks out their help, though his speech and actions show no respect for them: 'secret, black and midnight hags', 'filthy hags'.

The apparitions which rise out of the cauldron show one meaning to Macbeth but another in reality; the danger posed by Macduff seems to be wiped out by the second prediction which convinces Macbeth that he is invincible. He never quite interprets what the appearances of these apparitions signify – failing even to note that the child king has the detached branch of a tree in his hand. Perhaps these lapses in perception show how much his mind has deteriorated and the witches merely nudge him towards his downfall.

Where to find more help

Collins KS3 English Total Revision has a whole chapter on 'Reading and Writing about Shakespeare'. This chapter is suitable for you to read no matter which Shakespeare play you are studying or which level you are working at. It shows you how to improve your reading and writing skills and so move your Test answer to a higher level.

Chapter 21 of *Collins KS3 English Total Revision* gives you detailed guidance on 'Test Techniques Paper 2' which you need to develop in order to tackle the Shakespeare play successfully.

Two further Test practice tasks on 'Macbeth' can be found in Chapter 23 of *Collins KS3 English Total Revision*, with help and guidance in Chapter 28.

Twelfth Night
Task 5

Level 4

Understanding 6–8 marks

A level 4 answer will show a general understanding of how Malvolio was, by the device of the letter, tricked into behaving in a way that made him look ridiculous. Maria knows how strangely Malvolio is going to behave before he comes to Olivia's garden, and so she enjoys it immensely when he comes in smiling, behaving cheerfully and quoting from the letter. He also behaves towards Sir Toby and Fabian according to what the letter said. A level 4 answer will show a general understanding of the reason for Sir Andrew sending his aggressive challenge to Cesario so that this, as it is managed by Sir Toby, makes him look ridiculous.

Writing Skills 4–6 marks

The ideas showing understanding of both humorous situations will be clearly expressed. Sentences will be properly constructed with full stops and capital letters, and other punctuation within the sentences will be correctly used. Simple words will be spelt correctly and handwriting will be reasonably clear.

Typical remarks in a level 4 answer:

I have never laughed so much as the afternoon when my lady Olivia was a bit on edge because she was waiting for Cesario, and wanted to know where Malvolio was. I told her that he was coming, but was behaving very strangely, and secretly I knew why: it was that letter we had left him in Olivia's garden. Now he was falling for it and doing what it said. Sure enough, he came in smiling, which he never usually did, and dressed in yellow stockings which were cross-gartered. Olivia just thought he was mad, and told me to get him seen to before she went off to see Cesario. Sir Toby and Fabian came to poke fun at him and then, as if we hadn't had enough laughs for one day,

Sir Andrew came in with a challenge he was going to send to Cesario. Well, you just can't imagine the threats he was making, and Sir Toby agreed to give it to him, although when Sir Andrew had gone, Sir Toby said he would just tell him of the challenge. So, not only were we having fun with Malvolio acting in a ridiculous way, but we were going to see Sir Andrew challenge a bright-faced youth, when we all knew he couldn't fight a fly.

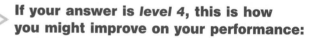

How to improve your level

▷ **If your answer is *level 4*, this is how you might improve on your performance:**

1 Do not just give a very general description of events as in the level 4 answer given. Give a **more detailed** explanation of why the two situations are funny and refer to the instructions in the letter and the language of the challenge to show why this is so.

2 Relate the characters to the situation, showing that Malvolio's dress and behaviour are so ridiculous because normally he is a very solemn and pompous character who never smiles or makes any affectionate gestures, and is always dressed in severe black. Point out that Sir Andrew's challenge is so funny because he himself is such a fop and a coward that he could never attack anybody.

3 Try to expand your vocabulary and make it more precise, and vary your sentence structure. Keep checking your spelling and punctuation, so that your meaning is quite clear. Write in paragraphs.

Level 5

Understanding   *10–12 marks*

At level 5, there will be more detail given about both situations so that the reasons for the humour, from Maria's point of view, will be clear. When the detailed situations are described with reference to Malvolio's superior and solemn character, and to Sir Andrew's foppish, pretentious and pathetic character, a much better understanding will be shown.

Writing Skills   *7–9 marks*

There will be a clear arrangement of paragraphs, reasonably varied sentence structure and a good range of vocabulary. There will be more precision in the choice of words and phrases to express the ideas. Punctuation will be accurate, especially the use of inverted commas, because now quotations will be included in the answer. Spelling of simple and more complex words will be correct.

Typical remarks in a level 5 answer:

I have never laughed so much in one afternoon. I knew we were going to have a good laugh when my lady Olivia, being a bit tense because she was expecting Cesario, asked for Malvolio because she wanted his sad and civil influence. I warned her that he was at present acting very strangely, but did not say why – of course, it was that letter that we had dropped for him to find in Olivia's garden.

Sure enough, when I had fetched him, he was dressed in yellow stockings and cross garters, bowing, smiling and kissing his hand, just as had been said in the letter. He even thought my lady wanted to go to bed with him. Well! Then he carried on quoting phrases from the letter which, of course, left Olivia totally bewildered, and she said he was suffering from 'midsummer madness'. Before she went to see Cesario, she told me to get Sir Toby to take special care of him.

What a person to choose! He was in on the trick!

Of course, I knew how Malvolio would behave while I had gone to fetch Sir Toby. He remained aloof and superior: 'Go off, I discard you.'

Sir Toby said he had plans to have him tied up in a dark room, but the next thing we knew was that Sir Andrew arrived, having written a challenge for a duel with Cesario. Sir Toby read it out, and, really, you never heard such violent and threatening language. This was all the funnier, because everyone knows that Sir Andrew could not attack anybody.

How to improve your level

> **If your answer is *level 5*, this is how you might improve on your performance:**

1 The level 5 answer given is a good narrative, telling the story of the scene. Although there are comments on the characters of Malvolio and Sir Andrew, you can develop this aspect further. The characters are placed in a situation which emphasises the faults in their make-up: Malvolio's arrogance and self-importance, and Sir Andrew's bluster and empty vanity.

2 Explain the 'dramatic irony', which is achieved because of some characters not knowing all that is going on, but the audience knowing everything. Malvolio's speech and behaviour are so funny because Olivia has no idea what he is doing and why; Sir Andrew is so vain that he does not know himself, or what the other characters think of him.

3 Think of different ways of expressing your ideas, and concentrate on choosing the exact word and phrase you need. Continue to use quotations, and make sure that spelling, punctuation and sentence construction are accurate.

How well did you do?

Level 6

Understanding   *14–16 marks*

At level 6, there is a development from the detailed narrative to an answer which has the same amount of detail and quotation, but which also has more critical comment about the humour of the play, about the characters it is based on, and about the effect of the humour. Sir Andrew's empty vanity and Malvolio's arrogant self-importance will be seen as the reasons for their becoming the targets of the humour. The way that some characters are unaware of what is happening will be pointed out by Maria, although, obviously, she cannot use the critical term, 'dramatic irony'.

Writing Skills   *10–12 marks*

The clarity of the expression will be helped by good paragraphing and a style where words and phrases will be precisely chosen. The vocabulary will be reasonably wide and all punctuation will be correct. Spelling of all but the most difficult words will be accurate, and handwriting will be well-formed and clear.

Typical remarks in a level 6 answer:

I have never laughed so much in one afternoon. My lady, Olivia, had made herself rather tense and nervous because she was waiting for Cesario to arrive, and she thought that the 'sad and civil' Malvolio would dampen down her excitement. I knew we would have some fun when she called for him, and in fact I warned her that he had such a 'very strange manner' that I was sure he was 'tainted in's wits'.
Olivia was shocked by his yellow stockings and cross garters and his habit of kissing his own hand. Of course, she was quite bewildered by his quoting from the letter that we had dropped for him earlier, and one of the funniest things I have ever seen was my lady's reactions to all his statements. She kept asking him questions, because she

How well did you do?

had no idea about the letter. In the end, she asked me to get Sir Toby to take 'special care' of him.
Malvolio, of course, had no idea that it was his very arrogance that we found so funny, and he maintained this to the end:
        'Go hang yourselves all!
Then there came Sir Andrew, another man so overbearing and pompous that he has no idea how we all think that he is pitifully weak and vain. Sir Toby read out this ridiculously violent challenge that he wanted to issue to Cesario – ridiculous, because Sir Andrew could not possibly carry it out.

How to improve your level

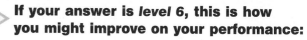

If your answer is *level 6*, this is how you might improve on your performance:

1   Remember that Maria is all-seeing and all-knowing, and so, in your answer, make her slip in phrases all the time about: the pompous and conceited character of Malvolio; the helpless confusion of Olivia, while at the same time she has to pretend to be in control; the irresponsibility of Sir Toby, although he is trusted by Olivia and Sir Andrew; and the pompous weakness of Sir Andrew who lacks self-knowledge and knowledge of the other characters.

2   Try to make some comment on the language of the characters – that is, not just what they say in appropriate quotations, but how they say it, in accordance with their character.

3   Organisation, accuracy and precision are what you need to aim at in your writing. Clear paragraphing, and accuracy of spelling and punctuation are vital. Think of alternative words and phrases to express a particular idea, and then select the most precise one.

How well did you do?

Level 7

Understanding   *18–22 marks*

A level 7 answer will include all the aspects that have been shown in increasing amounts through the other levels: **textual detail** in description of the events; quotations to illustrate the points being made; **critical comment** on the play's humour; **insight** into the characters, and how the humour springs from those characters as they are set in the dramatic situations. All this will be communicated to the reader by casual comments consistent with the character of Maria.

Writing Skills   *13–16 marks*

The style will be fluent and sufficiently well-organised to convince the reader – by choice of effective vocabulary and sentence structure – that this really is Maria speaking. Paragraphs will be used to make ideas and their illustrations clear. Spelling of simple and complex words will be correct, all punctuation will be accurate, and the handwriting will be well-formed and easy to read.

Typical remarks in a level 7 answer:

I have never laughed so much in one afternoon. My lady Olivia, being rather tense because she was anticipating the arrival of Cesario, asked for Malvolio because she thought he would create a sad and solemn atmosphere. I did warn her, though, that he was acting in a 'very strange manner' and that indeed he was 'tainted in's wits'. Although she was forewarned, Olivia was shocked:

> *'Smil'st thou? I sent for thee upon a sad occasion.'*

I could scarcely contain my mirth when Malvolio thought Olivia was offering to go to bed with him instead of advising him to rest. The very thought! It just shows how out of touch Malvolio is. He didn't even realise how bewildered Olivia was when he continued to quote phrases from the letter which we had

How well did you do?

dropped for him to find in Olivia's garden. The whole incident was so outrageous because Olivia had no idea why Malvolio was posturing and quoting the phrases, and Malvolio had no idea why she was so distraught.

As she concluded that it was 'midsummer madness', Cesario arrived and Olivia went off to see him, telling me to get Sir Toby to take 'a special care of him'. Sir Toby had conspired with me to work the trick, and so he relished the situation, pretending that he would 'deal gently with him' because he was possessed by devils. In fact, Sir Toby planned to confine him to a dark room so that we could have more fun by teasing him.

The fun continued when Sir Andrew arrived with a challenge he was going to issue to Cesario, because he was jealous of Olivia paying him so much attention. Sir Andrew made such a fool of himself in our eyes because his threats were so exaggerated that the difference between them and Sir Andrew's ability to put them into effect was hilarious.

Where to find more help

Collins KS3 English Total Revision has a whole chapter on 'Reading and Writing about Shakespeare'. This chapter is suitable for you to read no matter which Shakespeare play you are studying or which level you are working at. It shows you how to improve your reading and writing skills and so move your Test answer to a higher level.

Chapter 21 of *Collins KS3 English Total Revision* also gives you detailed guidance on 'Test Techniques Paper 2' which you need to develop in order to tackle the Shakespeare play successfully.

Two further Test practice tasks on 'Twelfth Night' can be found in Chapter 23 of *Collins KS3 English Total Revision*, with help and guidance in Chapter 29.

Twelfth Night
Task 6

How well did you do?

Level 4

Understanding   6–8 marks

A level 4 answer will concentrate on what happens in the scene, rather than writing about Olivia's feelings towards the three characters. The answer will describe what Olivia reacts to, rather than her reactions. In other words, the answer may state that Malvolio tries to persuade Olivia that the Clown is a bad fool and that Sir Toby is drunk, belching and being silly. After Maria has been sent out, Olivia spends a long time talking about beauty with Viola, whom she thinks is a man: there will be little comment on this part of the scene. There may be occasional rather weak comments on her feelings for each of the characters.

Writing Skills   4–6 marks

The expression will be clear enough for the pupil's meaning to be understood. Sentences will be properly constructed, with full stops and capital letters in the right places. Other punctuation will be correct, although there will probably be no paragraphing. There will be a narrow range of vocabulary, with no complex words, but the simple words will usually be spelled correctly. Handwriting will be clear and legible.

Typical remarks in a level 4 answer:

> *First, Olivia is speaking with Malvolio, and we know he hates the Clown, so he is telling Olivia that he is a really bad fool, not worth keeping in her household. Olivia does not agree with him, and is telling Malvolio so, when they are interrupted with the news that there is a young man at the gate who will not go away. Olivia also asks Sir Toby who is at the gate but she gets no sense out of him because he is drunk and silly and she has no patience with him. In the end, Viola comes in, but Olivia will not give her (him) proper answers. When she says who she is and Viola has obviously come with a message from Orsino, Olivia loses patience*

How well did you do?

> *again. But she sends Maria out and talks with Viola for a while because she thinks he is a man and she likes him.*

How to improve your level

▷ **If your answer is *level 4*, this is how you might improve on your performance:**

1 Begin with the way Olivia feels, because this is what the question asks, and do not waste time just saying what is happening when each of the characters appears. It is clear that Olivia doesn't much like Malvolio and argues with him and insults him. She has little patience with Sir Toby because of his unreasonable behaviour. At first, she tries to put off Viola, and will not give sensible answers, but later is much more interested in her (him).

2 You will naturally begin to describe Olivia's feelings if you think of the characters of the three people she speaks with. Their characters produce the feelings in her. Malvolio is miserable, selfish and critical of other people. Sir Toby is silly and irresponsible. Viola is bright, witty and very attentive to Olivia.

3 Check all your spelling and make sure your punctuation, including the full stops, is correct so that the reader can clearly understand what you want to say. Try to expand your vocabulary and vary the length of your sentences. Write in paragraphs: you could begin a new paragraph for each of the three characters, or use more than one paragraph when you are writing about Viola.

How well did you do?

Level 5

Understanding   *10–12 marks*

A level 5 answer will begin to describe the feelings of Olivia, as the question asks. This will be possible because now there will be more understanding shown of the characters of Malvolio, Sir Toby and Viola. It will be mostly a straightforward account, but there will be some references to the text, and some words or phrases used by the characters may be quoted.

Writing Skills   *7–9 marks*

The ideas will be organised clearly in paragraphs. There will be reasonably varied sentence structure, and vocabulary will be chosen effectively. A range of punctuation, including capital letters, full stops, commas, apostrophes and quotation marks, will be used accurately. Spelling, even of complex words, will usually be accurate, and handwriting will be clear and fluent.

Typical remarks in a level 5 answer:

When Olivia asks Malvolio for his opinion of the fool, Malvolio criticises him and says that he is worse than an average court fool. Olivia gets rather impatient with the way Malvolio hates everyone, and tells him that it is the fool's job to be silly and light-hearted. She soon sends Malvolio to deal with the man at the gate who will not go away.

As soon as she sees Sir Toby coming, Olivia can tell that he is drunk. He belches and deliberately misunderstands her words. She shows what she thinks of him by discussing his behaviour with the fool immediately after he has gone.

When Viola is finally brought in, Olivia is quite distant with him because she does not admit that she is the lady of the house. After she has admitted who she is, Viola flatters her by saying she has 'unmatchable beauty'. But Viola will not deliver the message, in spite of the fact that Olivia is rather stern: 'Tell me your mind.' However, the audience can see that Olivia is curious to know more

How well did you do?

about her visitor when she sends Maria out, so they are alone. She almost dismisses him when she hears that he is from Orsino, but then is interested enough to remove her veil and reveal her face.

Then there follows much praise of Olivia's beauty and the idea of Viola taking Orsino's place really appeals to her and at line 279 she says that she hopes Viola will return. After Viola has gone, Olivia reflects on what she said, and even sends Malvolio after her with a ring, saying it had been left. This is only an excuse to get Viola to return because, of course, Olivia thinks she is a man, and everything she has said and done in the last part of the scene shows that she feels a very strong attraction to him (her).

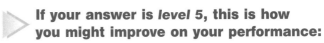

How to improve your level

If your answer is *level 5*, this is how you might improve on your performance:

1 Go into some detail with your comments on Olivia's feelings and the characters that she speaks with. Explore her reactions to Viola rather than just describing what happens when they meet: show a full understanding of their characters.

2 Include the most significant quotations as you explore these characters. Use the quotations which best express the most important feelings of Olivia towards the others.

3 Make sure you begin a new paragraph each time you deal with a new character, and also when Olivia changes and develops her feelings towards Viola. Check that your punctuation – capital letters, full stops, commas, apostrophes and quotation marks – is correct. Check that your spelling, even of the more difficult words, is accurate. Make sure your handwriting is easy to read.

How well did you do?

Level 6

Understanding   14–16 marks

A level 6 answer will give a more detailed account of the developing relationship between Olivia and Viola. More significant quotations will be used, especially in relation to what Olivia says. The significance of sending Malvolio with the ring at the end of the scene will be understood.

Writing Skills   10–12 marks

The writing will be accurate and well-organised in sentences and paragraphs. All aspects of punctuation will be correct, as will the spelling, even of more difficult words. There will be an attempt at precisely chosen vocabulary and phraseology rather than more colloquial expression. Handwriting will be fluent and clear.

Typical remarks in a level 6 answer:

Olivia is so exasperated at Malvolio's unforgiving nature that she expresses her genuine opinion of his character when she says: 'O! You are sick of self-love, Malvolio, and taste with a distempered appetite'.

Of course, Sir Toby is of no help in saying who the man is at the gate. He is belching and misunderstanding words, and Olivia can see that 'he's in the third degree of drink.' She takes no notice of him.

Because she refuses to be denied, Viola, dressed as Cesario, is finally allowed in to see Olivia.

When Viola remains polite and persistent, Olivia becomes curious about her (him), as she (he) seems so secretive: 'What I am, and what I would, are as secret as maidenhead.' This so intrigues Olivia that she sends Maria out and unveils her face. This naturally gives rise to more praise of her beauty and Olivia gives witty replies, being by now determined to engage him in conversation. In this conversation, they both appear to talk about Orsino, but make ambiguous suggestions about their increasingly strong

How well did you do?

attraction for each other. Olivia gives away her strong feelings when she invites Viola back again:
> *'Get to your lord:*
> *I cannot love him. Let him send no more,*
> *Unless, perchance, you come to me again'.*

So strong are her feelings that she tries to make sure that he (she) returns by sending Malvolio after him (her) with a ring which Olivia says he (she) left, but the audience knows that this is not true. So there is already revealed an affection for Viola (Cesario) which will be important later in the play.

How to improve your level

▷ **If your answer is *level 6*, this is how you might improve on your performance:**

1 Give as full and detailed an answer as possible, concentrating especially on Olivia's thoughts and feelings, and showing how they change during the conversation with Viola. Malvolio's most important speech is at the beginning of the part of the scene you have to study, from line 81. Show that the other characters and the audience agree with Olivia's opinion of him.

2 A few, brief lines of speech, and questions, can be used to indicate Olivia's feelings about each character. Quote these and comment on their significance, especially those relating to Viola. Show that these at first hide, and then reveal, her developing feelings towards Viola (Cesario).

3 Present your answer in clearly arranged paragraphs, each of which covers an obviously different topic. Write accurately and with some sense of style.

How well did you do?

Level 7

Understanding 18–22 marks

A level 7 answer will be full of detail and quotation, all of which will be relevant to Olivia's feelings towards Malvolio, Sir Toby and Viola. Her feelings will be described not as if they remain unchanging, but as they develop and respond to the character with whom she is talking. There will be a good deal of insight into each character as he or she relates to Olivia, so that her feelings can be shown as reactions to those characters. Well-selected quotations will illustrate her feelings, and they will always support statements which are direct responses to the question.

Writing Skills 13–16 marks

The writing will be confident, accurate and well-organised. The length of sentences will vary, but each one will be carefully constructed for a particular purpose. The paragraphs will reflect each step in the development of Olivia's feelings. Punctuation will be used correctly in order to make the sequence of ideas and feelings clear. Spelling, including that of complex words, will be accurate, and handwriting will be fluent and regular.

Typical remarks in a level 7 answer:

Although it is true that Olivia invites Malvolio's opinion of the Clown, she is utterly exasperated at his relentless and destructively critical attitude. She realises that this is because Malvolio has no sympathy for the Clown or anyone else, and that this in turn is because he is obsessed with himself. Her analysis of him, therefore, is: 'O! You are sick of self-love, Malvolio, and taste with a distempered appetite.' That is, his total concern with his self-importance always puts the worst interpretation on anyone else's behaviour, however innocent or well-meaning. This is very perceptive of Olivia and has implications for the treatment of Malvolio later in the play.

The audience has seen Sir Toby before, and is not surprised at his crude and

How well did you do?

offensive behaviour, as he belches and distorts Olivia's words with rude interpretations. Olivia treats him with amused tolerance, knowing that 'he's in the third degree of drink'.

Although Olivia pretends innocence when Viola, disguised as Cesario, is finally allowed to see her, she knew from the beginning that he (she) had come from Orsino. In a rather distant and aloof way, she toys with him (her) with a series of terse questions about who he (she) is and what he (she) wants. She is not at all impressed by his (her) effusive praise - 'Most radiant, exquisite, and unmatchable beauty' - and says, bluntly:

'Come to what is important in't: I forgive you the praise.'

In the face of Cesario's (Viola's) courtesy and persistence, however, Olivia engages him (her) in conversation. She is quick to appreciate that he is deliberately ambiguous in his statements: 'What I am, and what I would, are as secret as maidenhead'. After she has dismissed Maria and unveiled her face, his (her) praise of Olivia's beauty is clearly intended to come from him (her) as much as from Orsino, whom he represents. Olivia reciprocates his (her) feelings by distinguishing between him (her) and his (her) master:

> *'Get you to your lord:*
> *I cannot love him. Let him send no more,*
> *Unless, perchance, you come to me again,*
> *To tell me how he takes it.'*

The sending of Malvolio with a ring that he (she) has supposedly left behind (although the audience know better) betrays the strength of Olivia's attraction to him (her). Indeed, she is surprised at her own feelings:

> *'Even so quickly may one catch the plague?*
> *Methinks I feel this youth's perfections*
> *With an invisible and subtle stealth*
> *To creep in at mine eyes.'*

ENGLISH TEST
ADDITIONAL PAPER ①

Reading and Writing

Section A

Read the following story.

Then answer all the questions which follow it.

The story describes an incident with a wild pig (or peccary), which is one of the rare animals Gerald Durrell is collecting in the jungles of South America.

'Did you get it?' I inquired hopefully.

'Yes, thank you,' said Bob, 'and we've been trying to keep it in this blessed box ever since we left the village. Apparently it doesn't like being shut up. I thought it was meant to be tame. In fact, I remember you telling me it was a tame one. That was the only reason I agreed to go and fetch it.'   5

'Well, the boy said it was tame.'

'The boy, bless him, was mistaken,' said Bob coldly; 'the brute appears to be suffering from claustrophobia.'

Gingerly we carried the box from the boat to the beach.

'You'd better watch out,' warned Bob, 'it's already got some of the slats loose on top.'   10

As he spoke the peccary leapt inside the box and hit the top like a sledgehammer; the slats flew off like rockets, and the next minute a bristling and enraged pig had hauled himself out and was galloping up the beach, snorting savagely.

'There!' said Bob, 'I knew that would happen.'

Half-way up the beach the peccary met a small group of Amerindians. He rushed among   15
them, squealing with rage, trying to bite their legs; his sharp, half-inch tusks clicked together at each bite. The Amerindians fled back to the village, hotly pursued by the pig, who was in turn being chased by Ivan and myself. When we reached the huts the inhabitants appeared to have vanished, and the peccary was having a quick snack off some mess he had found under a palm tree. We had rounded the corner of a hut and come upon him rather   20
unexpectedly, but he did not hesitate for a minute. Leaving his meal he charged straight towards us with champing mouth, uttering a bloodcurdling squeal. The next few moments were crowded, with the peccary twirling round and round, chopping and squealing, while Ivan and I leapt madly about with the speed and precision of a well-trained corps de ballet. At last the pig decided we were too agile for him, and he retreated into a gap between   25
two of the huts and stood there grunting derisively at us.

'You go round and guard the other end, Ivan,' I panted. 'I'll see he doesn't get away this side.'

Ivan disappeared round the other side of the huts, and I saw Mr Kahn waddling over the sand towards me. I was filled with an unholy glee. 30

'Mr Kahn,' I called. 'Can you come and help for a minute?'

'Sure, Chief,' he said, beaming. 'What you want?'

'Just stand here and guard this opening, will you? There's a peccary in there and I don't want him to get out. I'll be back in a second.'

35

Leaving Mr Kahn peering doubtfully at the peccary, I rushed over to our hut and unearthed a thick canvas bag, which I wrapped carefully round my left hand. Thus armed I returned to the scene of the fray. To my delight I was just in time to see Mr Kahn panting flatfootedly round the palm trees with the peccary close behind. To my disappointment the peccary stopped chasing Mr Kahn as soon as he saw me and retreated once more between the huts.

40

'Golly!' said Mr Kahn. 'That pig's plenty fierce, Chief.'

He sat down in the shade and fanned himself with a large red handkerchief, while I squeezed my way between the huts and moved slowly towards the peccary. He stood quite still, watching me, champing his jaws occasionally and giving subdued grunts. He let me get within six feet of him, and then he charged. As he reached me I grabbed the bristly scruff of his neck with my right hand and plunged my left, encased in canvas, straight into his mouth. He champed his jaws desperately, but his tusks made no impression through the canvas. I shifted my grip, got my arm firmly round his fat body and lifted him off the ground. As soon as he felt himself hoisted into the air his confidence seemed to evaporate, he stopped biting my hand and started squeaking in the most plaintive manner, kicking out with his fat little hind legs. I carried him over to our hut and deposited him in a box that was strong enough to hold him. Soon he had his snout buried in a dish full of chopped bananas and milk and was snorting and squelching with satisfaction. Never again did he show off and try to be the Terror of the Jungle; in fact he became absurdly tame. A glimpse of his feeding dish would send him into squealing transports of delight, a frightful song that would only end when his nose was deep in the dish and his mouth full of food. He adored being scratched, and if you continued this treatment for long enough he would heel over and fall flat on his side, lying motionless, with his eyes tightly closed and giving tiny grunts of pleasure. We christened him Percy, and even Bob grew quite fond of him, though I suspect that the chief reason for this was that he had seen him chasing Mr Kahn round the palm trees.

45

50

55

60

From *Three Singles to Adventure* by Gerald Durrell

Section A

Answer the following questions.

1   **From the beginning, we know that the peccary is not tame. Pick out two pieces of evidence from the first conversation which tell us this.**

6 marks

2   **Describe the plan which the narrator carried out to catch the escaped pig.**

In your answer, comment on:

*   how Mr Kahn was used as a decoy;

*   how the narrator protected himself from the peccary's tusks;

*   how the animal was finally caught.

11 marks

Section B

Read the pieces called 'Driven Crazy' (page 63) and 'The Ultimate Nightmare' (pages 64–65) and then complete the following task.

3   **Explain how the two pieces express some of the problems which modern traffic is creating, both in central London and to non-drivers.**

In your answer you need to consider:

*   the information in the boxes and the chart, including facts and figures;

*   the layout of the two pieces.

11 marks

Adrian Davis reports on what the future may hold for non-car users – Britain's dying breed.

Driven crazy

Travel by car is less safe per mile travelled than all forms of public transport – boats, planes, trains and buses. Yet we are becoming increasingly reliant on the car.

Mobility is becoming so important and cars pose such a threat to other, more vulnerable road users, particularly the elderly and young, pedestrians and cyclists, that many people who might prefer to walk or pedal have succumbed to driving. The Department of Transport claims that more and more elderly people, women and ethnic minorities are joining the motorists' ranks.

Over the next 35 years, according to the Department, traffic levels may increase by as much as two and a half times present levels. Growth on such a scale will almost inevitably result in more deaths and injuries and the further intimidation of non-motorised travellers. But instead of seeing road safety as a public health problem, the Department of Health seems to be leaving accident prevention to the Department of Transport, which is currently consulting on proposals to improve pedestrian safety.

Last year 5,041 people were killed on the roads, of whom 39 per cent were pedestrians and cyclists, and 95,000 more casualties occupied hospital beds. In 1987 out of 311,473 road traffic casualties, 1,703 pedestrians died as a result of their injuries. The number of minor injuries sustained can only be guessed at since a vast proportion never gets reported.

A survey by the Transport and Road Research Laboratory 10 years ago found that pedestrian accident victims stayed in hospital longer on average than vehicle occupants. The most common types of injuries are to the head and legs, followed by arms, chest and pelvis.

According to the Parliamentary Advisory Council for Transport Safety (Pacts), the cost of pedestrian casualties is estimated at over £1 billion. Mrs Jeanne Breen, Pacts co-ordinator, reports that 95 per cent of casualties occur in urban and residential areas, where there is strong justification for safety and traffic flow to be balanced more effectively.

Although 80 per cent of journeys under one mile are made on foot, walking half a mile to the shops is seen as unimportant in terms of road planning. As Dr Mayer Hillman of the Policy Studies Institute points out, the National Travel Survey is used to recognise changing trends in motorised travel. Road safety for pedestrians takes second place.

What does the projected growth in traffic volume mean for the public health? It means that life for those who cannot afford a car will become increasingly unbearable as streets become more congested and polluted. Surveys already suggest that less than one-fifth of all children takes enough exercise to maintain or improve health and the only exercise many adults take is walking to and from work and the shops.

But as more roads carve up the community and more of us are forced into the motor car we will soon require pedestrian sanctuaries for exercise purposes – to which we will doubtless have to drive!

Adrian Davis is London Road Safety Co-ordinator of Friends of the Earth.

The Guardian
23 August 1989

THE ULTIMATE

PINCHPOINTS
Motorways narrowing into trunk roads form classic pinchpoints. One of the worst pinchpoints in the south-east occurs where the six-lane M2 narrows and becomes the four-lane A2

DELIVERIES
Commercial vehicles travel a total of 11 million miles every working day in Greater London. Although lorries would cause less congestion if they delivered at night, residents in many parts of the country are protected by night-time bans on lorries

TRAFFIC SPEEDS IN CENTRAL LONDON

SOURCE: GLC SURVEY OF
WORST-PEAK-TIME AVERAGE SPEEDS

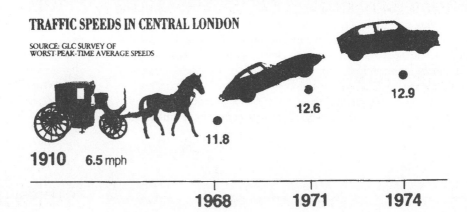

1910   **6.5** mph

11.8

12.6

12.9

1968   **1971**   **1974**

NIGHTMARE

JUNCTIONS
Britain's most vulnerable junction is at the bottom of Park Lane in London; a traffic lights failure there at rush hour will block Victoria, Westminster and Marble Arch within 20 minutes

CONTRAFLOWS
Contraflows increase the risk of accidents one-and-half times. The most notorious contraflow, between junctions 11 and 13 of the M25, has been in place for four months and will remain for another 18 months

BUSES AND TAXIS
Although buses carry over five-and-half million passengers each year, they often occupy a separate lane, limiting the progress of other traffic. The 39,000 licensed taxis in Britain stop every 20 minutes, adding to congestion

ROAD WORKS
Gas, electricity and water boards last year dug two million holes between them. Although 1960s motorways were built with a life expectancy of just 25 years, Government funding restricts repairs to under 80 miles of network a year

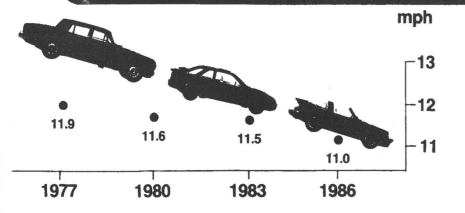

mph

- 13
- 12
- 11

11.9   11.6   11.5   11.0

1977   **1980**   **1983**   **1986**

© The Daily Telegraph plc, London 24 September 1988

Section C

This section is a test of your ability to write clearly and accurately in your own style using:

* *paragraphs;*
* *a range of sentence structures and vocabulary;*
* *correct spelling and punctuation.*

Aim to write about two pages.

You may use notepaper to help you plan your answer.

Whichever task you choose, your writing can be true or imaginary.

Choose ONE of the following:

4   EITHER

(a) **Write about how to look after any one pet animal, and describe the pleasure this gives, as well as the demands it makes.**

You could write about:

* how you like the things you have to do;
* how you like the way the animal treats you;
* how much it takes of your time, money, effort.

OR

(b) **You are walking alone at night in a neighbourhood you know well. Suddenly, you hear a groan and then a voice calling 'Help!' Write the story.**

OR

(c) You have read many articles in magazines which state that cars are a danger to pedestrians, cause pollution and congest town centres.

Imagine that you are a mother of two small children, and write, in a letter to a newspaper, that you are tired of anti-car arguments.

Write the letter from your home address. Begin 'Dear Sir' and end with 'Yours faithfully' and your signature.

In your letter, you could mention the convenience of a car to you in:

* saving time;
* shopping;
* transporting your children about;
* looking after elderly parents.

Answers and Tutorials
Additional Paper 1
Sections A and B

HOW TO MARK YOUR ANSWERS

How well did you do?

For each question, there is a description of the **type of answer** that Test Examiners would expect to see at each level. Also included are examples of **typical remarks** that students would be likely to include at each level.

Read through each of your answers several times to see if you can match it up to the level where it seems to fit best.

If you are unsure, ask someone you can trust – a relative or friend – to help you.

How to improve your level

Once you have decided what level your answer is, look at the column headed 'How to improve your level'. This suggests what you need to do to improve your skill so that you can give a better answer next time – and achieve a higher level.

Where to find more help

This section includes detailed references to *Collins KS3 English Total Revision*. Whichever level you are working at in your reading, this book will help you to develop the skills you need.

Additional Paper 1
Section A Question 1

How well did you do?	How to improve your level

Level 4   *2 marks*

With the reading passage, there are always two questions – a short, easier one with a few marks, and a longer, harder one with more marks. Therefore, when you are actually doing the test, it is advisable not to spend too long on the shorter question which has fewer marks.

Here, the first question is the easier one, and a Level 4 answer will manage to pick out the most important or most obvious parts of the passage to answer the question. What has to be shown is that the pig (peccary) is not tame, and the part of the passage you need to look at is the first conversation. A level 4 answer will not, however, concentrate exactly on 'two pieces of evidence'. It will probably not give any quotations and will be a bit vague.

Typical remarks in a level 4 answer:

> *We know the peccary is not tame because Bob said the boy had been mistaken, and the boy said it was tame. He also said it had got some slats loose.*

If your answer is *level 4*, this is how you might improve on your performance:

1 Do not give only the most obvious pieces of evidence for the point you are trying to prove, but search for all evidence, including the evidence which is only hinted at.

2 If the question refers to a conversation, give actual quotations from the conversation, and do not be vague.

3 Except where you are quoting, answer in your own words.

4 Examine carefully each term in the question, and not only the most noticeable ones.

Level 5   *3 marks*

A level 5 answer will show a better understanding of what evidence really is. The evidence will be pinpointed and actual quotations from the conversation will be given, so that it will seem a more exact answer.

Typical remarks in a level 5 answer:

> *The fact that the peccary is not tame is indicated in the conversation by the fact that the person telling the story says, 'Well, the boy said it was tame', but then Bob, who had to capture it and transport it, said: 'The boy, bless him, was mistaken.' Bob also went on to say, about the pig, 'it's already got some slats loose on top'. These two pieces of evidence from the first conversation tell us that the peccary is not tame.*

If your answer is *level 5*, this is how you might improve on your performance:

1 What you have to show is *understanding* – so look for as much evidence as possible, direct and indirect, to demonstrate your understanding.

2 Organise your answers in such a way as to get as many points as possible into a reasonably short answer.

3 Although this question asks you to quote, write the rest of the answer in your own words.

4 Think about and comment on meanings behind the speech of characters in the story.

How well did you do?

Level 6
4 marks

A level 6 answer may include references to other suggestions, in the first conversation, that the peccary is not tame. There may be more subtle evidence found and used, and the answer may be more cleverly organised in order to include these additional pieces of evidence.

Typical remarks in a level 6 answer:

> *The fact that the peccary is not tame is first hinted at when Bob uses the phrase, 'this blessed box', and this is added to when he sarcastically says, 'I thought it was meant to be tame.' However, the best evidence is when Bob, on being told that the boy said it was tame, says, 'The boy ... was mistaken' and when he later says, 'it's already got some of the slats loose on top'.*

Level 7
5–6 marks

A level 7 answer will be developed further and will include more points in the same length of answer. In this way it will show a better understanding of the passage as a whole.

Typical remarks in a level 7 answer:

> *The first suggestion that the peccary is not tame is in Bob's exasperated use of the phrase, 'this blessed box'. The sarcasm in the sentence 'I thought it was meant to be tame' reinforces this impression. The conclusive evidence, though, is when Bob, on hearing of the boy's claim that it was tame, says, 'The boy ... was mistaken', and his later assertion: 'it's already got some of the slats loose on top'.*

How to improve your level

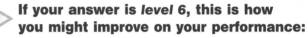 **If your answer is *level* 6, this is how you might improve on your performance:**

1 Search for all the evidence possible – subtle and suggestive, as well as clear and obvious – to show the high degree of your understanding.

2 Organise your answer in such a way that you include as many points as possible in a few short phrases. There are no marks for the style of your writing in answers to the reading passages, but the more concisely you write, the more points you can include.

3 Respond to the *tone* and *suggested* meanings of the passage. This will demonstrate how well you have understood what you have read.

Where to find more help

Collins KS3 English Total Revision has several units on 'Reading and Understanding Fiction':

Level 4 pages 1–3

Level 5 pages 17–21

Level 6 pages 39–43

Level 7 pages 60–64

Test practice on Paper 1 Section A is on pages 123–126; sample students' answers and examiner's comments are on pages 152–157.

Additional Paper 1
Section A Question 2

Level 4　　　　　　　　*3–4 marks*

The question says 'Describe the plan', but if you are to score good marks, the description will have to show an understanding of the characters involved and the method used. A level 4 answer will not show this understanding. It will just tell the story of how the plan is carried out, and will use phrases from the passage.

Typical remarks in a level 4 answer:

Leaving Mr Kahn guarding the peccary, the writer rushed over to his hut and got a thick canvas bag to wrap round his left hand. He went back in between the huts and moved slowly towards the peccary. He grabbed him by the neck and pushed his left hand in the bag into his mouth. Then he got his arm round his fat body, lifted him, carried him to the hut and put him in a box.

Level 5　　　　　　　　*5–6 marks*

A level 5 answer will not copy phrases from the passage, and will show more understanding of the characters involved and the method used. That is, the answer will follow the 'prompts' (the instructions underneath the main questions) and will develop them in detail.

Typical remarks in a level 5 answer:

The author left Mr Kahn to guard the peccary while he went to arm himself with a thick canvas bag. When he returned, Mr Kahn had let him go, but the author trapped the pig again between the huts, grabbed him by the neck with his right hand and stuffed his left hand, protected by the canvas bag, into his mouth. He then put his right arm round his body, lifted him, carried him back to his hut, and confined him in a box.

▷ **If your answer is *level 4*, this is how you might improve on your performance:**

1 Do not just follow the story of the plan as it is written in the passage, but arrange the ideas as you want, not being afraid to leave plenty out.

2 Do not copy phrases from the original passage, but think of your own words to describe the ideas which you need to include.

3 Although the question simply says 'Describe the plan', try to add explanations of your own to show that you understand what the author means by his description.

▷ **If your answer is *level 5*, this is how you might improve on your performance:**

1 Follow the 'prompts' – that is, the instructions which are printed in less bold type underneath the main question. They will show you the various different aspects you need to cover in your answer, and you need to give as many details on each aspect as you can.

2 Try to show a complete understanding of the whole situation – where everything is, where each person and animal is, the events that are going on and what is about to happen, and an explanation of it all.

3 Show that you appreciate the humour of the situation. You can do this by pointing out the details of the situation, and by your own choice of word and phrase.

How well did you do?

Level 6
7–8 marks

A level 6 answer will show fuller understanding of the whole situation, including characters and method of capture. There will also be a response to the humorous interlude involving Mr Kahn.

Typical remarks in a level 6 answer:

> *Although the author had left Mr Kahn guarding the peccary, while he went to arm himself with a thick canvas bag, Mr Kahn was not equal to this task and the author returned to see him being chased by the pig. However, he trapped him again between the huts and when he was close enough, the author grabbed the scruff of his neck with his right hand and pushed his left hand, protected by the canvas bag, into his mouth. By changing the grip of his right hand to encircle his body, he was able to lift the squeaking pig up, carry him over to his hut, and push him into a box from which he could not escape.*

How to improve your level

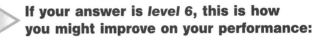

If your answer is *level 6*, this is how you might improve on your performance:

1 Further develop the improved aspects from Level 5 – adding details to the prompts, showing a complete understanding of the situation through the events, the characters and the humour, with explanations.

2 You will need to demonstrate your understanding of the plan by carefully choosing vocabulary to express your thoughts. In the example of a level 7 answer (page 72), notice how much thought and understanding of the situation are expressed by phrases like: 'the newly-escaped pig', the 'hopeless awkwardness' of Mr Kahn, the author being a 'more shrewd character', the 'protesting, whimpering, kicking pig'. The phrases do not have to be long and the words do not have to be complicated and elaborate, but they must be appropriate and informative.

3 Make sure your answer is well-organised by providing an opening statement, and leading up to your concluding thoughts with conviction. Try to make your answer as entertaining and satisfying as the original story. This can be done only by thoroughly absorbing and understanding all the details of the narrative in the original passage.

How well did you do?

Level 7
9–11 marks

A level 7 answer will show a still more fully developed understanding of the whole situation. Although no marks will be awarded for the *style* of the answer, a level 7 answer will use phrases which give a lot of information in a few words and which, in themselves, show a response to character and humour. A very good answer may be as entertaining as the original passage – because the student has thoroughly absorbed the content, structure and language of the passage.

Typical remarks in a level 7 answer:

Having left Mr Kahn guarding the peccary, the narrator expected him to cope while he went to arm himself with a thick canvas bag. On his return, though, he saw the newly-escaped pig chasing Mr Kahn, whose hopeless awkwardness is shown by the phrase, 'panting flatfootedly'. Quickly, the author, a much more shrewd character, trapped the pig between the huts again. He approached him closely, seized the scruff of his neck with his right hand while he forced his left, protected by the canvas bag, into his mouth. The bag saved him from injury by the sharp tusks. A deft manoeuvre with his right arm enabled him to encircle the pig's body. He then lifted the protesting, whimpering, kicking pig over to his hut and again imprisoned him in a box from which there was no escape.

Where to find more help

Collins KS3 English Total Revision has several units on 'Reading and Understanding Fiction':

Level 4 pages 1–3

Level 5 pages 17–21

Level 6 pages 39–43

Level 7 pages 60–64

Test practice on Paper 1 Section A is on pages 123–126; sample students' answers and examiner's comments are on pages 152–157.

Additional Paper 1
Section B Question 3

How well did you do?

Level 4 — *3–4 marks*

A level 4 answer will be mainly descriptive and general. It will list a few of the major traffic problems. The answer will show an awareness of the overall difference in styles between the two pieces. There will not be much reference to the text and no quotations will be used.

Typical remarks in a level 4 answer:

> *Today's main problems on roads are:*
> *Overcrowding, this means that roads are becoming blocked with traffic, making many important journeys, or really any journey slow. Cars are the most popular form of transport in central London.*
> *The other problem is pollution, fumes from cars, motorbikes, buses and lorries contain greenhouse gases that break down the ozone and may cause cancer to many pedestrians.*
> *The difference in the layout of the information is that one is a written document and the other is a graphic presentation, including diagrams and written information.*

Level 5 — *5–6 marks*

A level 5 answer will include an overview of the information and ideas in the material but the relevant points made will not always be linked to the texts. Comments about the layout will be specific and will identify some devices used, without being technical or giving examples.

Typical remarks in a level 5 answer:

> *Modern traffic causes many deaths to pedestrians, cyclists and other motorists. These deaths occur due to the large amount of traffic coming and going in London and also hazards such as traffic light failure, road works and contraflows. Costs for pedestrian casualties exceed £1 million. Most accidents which injure pedestrians are caused because motorists become less patient and more speedy to make up for lost time in traffic.*
> *In 'The Ultimate Nightmare' the information is laid out like a poster with the different pieces of information arranged separately.*

How to improve your level

▷ **If your answer is *level 4*, this is how you might improve on your performance:**

1 Look at the different aspects of the task as directed by the prompts; make sure you have covered the *content* (information) and the *style* (layout).

2 Include plenty of detail in your answer. Pick out the most important facts, write them in your own words, and then give authority to what you say by quoting the relevant piece from the original. Remember to put inverted commas (speech marks) round the words you copy.

▷ **If your answer is *level 5*, this is how you might improve on your performance:**

1 Try to expand on the general overview you have given by adding specific details from the text, supported by quotations (but do not make these too long).

2 Where you have noted a particular feature of the layout, give specific examples and try to say what the *effect* on the reader is.

3 You may personalise your answer by giving your own opinion as to which parts of the material you find the more effective, and say why.

> *It also has pictures showing the various hazards. 'Driven Crazy', however, is a newspaper article and instead of just stating the facts it explains them. There is more information in driven crazy but the ultimate nightmare is easier to understand.*

How well did you do?

Level 6
7–8 marks

A level 6 answer will show a more objective view of what each piece is trying to communicate. There will be appropriate references to language, content and layout, with suitable illustrations.

Typical remarks in a level 6 answer:

Modern traffic is causing problems for all road users, including non-drivers in central London. Mobility is so important but cars pose such a threat to others that, the more people that join the ranks of motorists, the more deaths and injuries there will be to non-motorised travellers. The Department of Transport is currently consulting on proposals to improve pedestrian safety, as over the next 35 years, traffic levels may increase by two and a half times present levels. Soon the only form of exercise we will take will be walking to and from the car.

Some of the main traffic problems are: pinchpoints – problems in that several lanes of traffic must fit into much less as motorways narrow towards city roads; junctions – one traffic light failure at a junction can cause havoc and queues; motorway contraflows – higher risk of accidents; buses and taxis – carry more people but special lanes stop other traffic flowing; deliveries – better made at night but local residents complain; road works – caused by mains services repairs and road maintenance.

Roughly the same messages are transmitted in both pieces, though one is continuous writing and one is partly pictorial, including a chart showing the increase and decrease in speed in central London caused by pressure of traffic. 'The Ultimate Nightmare' has the information scattered in front of you, whereas 'Driven Crazy' is organised into columns and paragraphs.

How to improve your level

If your answer is *level 6*, this is how you might improve on your performance:

1 You have the main ideas, so now try to be more analytical – perhaps focus on one of the statements you have made and explain why this is so.

2 Do not be afraid to make reference to the text without actually quoting from it; in this way you can often make points more neatly and show that you really have internalised what you have read.

3 Although you need to include the main facts in your answer, it shows more understanding to summarise than to slavishly copy lists of points made in the original.

How well did you do?

Level 7 — *9–11 marks*

A level 7 answer will be confident, detailed, and linked to the texts. It will show an understanding of the different *purposes* of the two pieces. Content and layout will be commented on effectively and in detail.

Typical remarks in a level 7 answer:

There are many problems created by modern traffic. We can categorise these into two groups, driver problems and pedestrian problems. The factors involved in the driver problems are road layout, the vehicles themselves and road works. Firstly, road layout: pinchpoints occur where motorways narrow into trunk roads; a good example of this is where the six-lane M2 turns into the four-lane A2, one of the worst pinchpoints in the south-east! Secondly, junctions – where two roads cross, accidents are prevented by placing traffic lights at the junction, but traffic light failure can result in accidents, or, in the case of the Park Lane junction, block a large portion of central London. Next, contraflows which can increase the risk of accidents significantly; the most notorious contraflow recently on the M25 was in operation for nearly two years! And then there are the vehicle problems: deliveries – commercial vehicles travel a total of 11 million miles in every working day, and that's just in Greater London, and they can't travel at night because in some places there is a night-time ban on lorries; buses and taxis, though carrying lots of people, cause congestion because their lanes limit the flow of other traffic, plus, they keep stopping. Finally, roadworks create massive disruption, caused mostly by mains servicing and road repairs. Hence, the average traffic speed in London has been decreasing since 1974, despite the increase over the same period in the car's capabilities.

The pedestrian troubles are a whole new problem; in 1988 alone 5,041 people were killed on the roads, 39 per cent of which were pedestrians or cyclists, and 95,000 more casualties occupied hospital beds.

How well did you do?

The two pieces were set out completely differently. 'The Ultimate Nightmare' was set out in an artistic way to grab the reader's attention. I think it did not work too successfully as it appeared a bit haphazard. In contrast, I found 'Driven Crazy' much more accessible, as it was well-structured, with far more data and information.

Where to find more help

Collins KS3 English Total Revision has several units on 'Reading and Understanding Non-Fiction':

Level 4 pages 4–6

Level 5 pages 22–25

Level 6 pages 44–47

Level 7 pages 65–68

Test practice on Paper 1 Section A is on pages 127–128; sample students' answers and examiner's comments are on pages 158–161.

Answers and Tutorials
Additional Paper 1
Section C

HOW TO MARK YOUR ANSWERS

How well did you do?

Examiners assess students' writing according to a range of different criteria:

1 *What* you write. Examiners judge the number and quality of your ideas – your imagination and originality.

2 The structure of your writing – for example, how you begin and end your essay, how varied your sentence structure is, how you divide your writing into paragraphs etc.

3 Expression and style. Examiners assess your choice of words and phrases. They look at how *exact* and appropriate your words are, and how you arrange your words and phrases into sentences and paragraphs.

4 How accurate your grammar, spelling and punctuation are, and how legible your handwriting is.

In order to work out what level you would be awarded for the essay you have written, you need to read through the general assessment guidance that is given for each level. This covers all the aspects mentioned above.

Also read carefully the typical sentences that an examiner would expect to see in an essay at each level. Your sentences will obviously not be the same – but you should be able to spot whether your writing shares the same characteristics.

See if you can match your essay up to the level where it seems to fit best. If you are unsure, ask someone you can trust – a relative or friend – to help you.

How to improve your level

Once you have decided what level your writing would be awarded, look at the column headed 'How to improve your level' which is alongside.

This suggests what you need to do to improve your writing skills so that you can write a better essay next time – and achieve a higher level.

Where to find more help

This section includes detailed references to *Collins KS3 English Total Revision*. Whichever level you are working at in your writing, this book will help you to develop the skills you need.

Additional Paper 1
Section C Question 4(a)

| **How well did you do?** | **How to improve your level** |

Level 4 *8–12 marks*

In all writing tests, people love to write stories. Although this writing task asks for some explanation, and for a balance of pleasures and demands, a level 4 answer will turn it all into a story. The writer may start by saying that a dog, for instance, gives pleasure by the happiness it shows when being taken for a walk. Then he or she may forget the balance necessary and just tell the story of a dog walk.

There will be very little descriptive detail in the answer. There will be no searching for exact words to describe what is meant, and the sentences will run on for so long that there will not be any real structure or control. There will be no paragraphing. The style may be colloquial – that is, writing as you speak. Punctuation and spelling may be poor because they have not been checked carefully.

Typical remarks in a level 4 answer:

> *My dog, Rex, loves being taken for a walk, and I have to take him for about an hour every day. Sometimes I like it, though. The other day, I was taking him down by the canal and he met another dog that he didn't like much, so they got to fighting and both fell in the water. Rex doesn't like water much, but after thrashing about a bit, they both climbed out and then carried on fighting.*

> **If your answer is *level 4*, this is how you might improve on your performance:**

1. Do not let sentences run on for so long that they are not properly controlled. Try to have a number of short sentences. Do not use 'so' to connect long phrases: this is not correct grammar.

2. Write in paragraphs. This is especially important in answer to a question like this because there are different aspects to the question and you must let the reader follow the development of each different aspect. Without paragraphs, this development will not be clear to the reader.

3. Try to choose exact words to express what you mean, and try to get away from the style in which you speak: instead of 'down by' write 'along'; instead of 'got to fighting' write 'started fighting'; instead of 'carried on' write 'continued'.

How well did you do?

Level 5 *14–18 marks*

A level 5 answer will show more ability to organise the ideas into well-ordered paragraphs, which is what the question asks for. These paragraphs may follow the 'prompts' (the extra instructions underneath the main question). In a task involving explanation and description such as this, there may be no speech used, which simplifies the punctuation, though full stops, capital letters, commas and apostrophes will be correctly placed. Spelling of all except the most difficult words will be correct. Handwriting will be legible and clearly formed.

Typical remarks in a level 5 answer:

When I originally asked if I could have a dog, my parents agreed, as long as I looked after all its needs myself.

They seemed to look on all the time that has to be spent looking after a dog as some kind of hard labour to be suffered in order to justify the pleasure of playing with him and stroking him as he snuggles up in front of the fire.

Certainly I have to spend a long time taking him for walks, buying his food, feeding him, bathing him, brushing him and sometimes taking him to the vet's. But this is not labour. I love it. He is my constant companion and I adore him.

How to improve your level

▷ **If your answer is *level 5*, this is how you might improve on your performance:**

1 A plan is essential for answers to this type of question. You will have to follow all three 'prompts' (the extra instructions below the main question) and there will be two or three paragraphs for each one. If you do not do this, you will have ignored part of the question and you will lose marks.

2 Search for exact words with which to express your information and thoughts.

3 Carry out a complete check of all spelling, punctuation and grammar, so that your writing is clear and fluent.

How well did you do?

Level 6   *20–24 marks*

In a level 6 answer the ideas will be well-organised in paragraphs, but they will also be expressed in some cleverly chosen words and phrases, which are included in well-constructed sentences. There will be a liveliness about the writing which holds the attention of the reader. Punctuation will be accurate, so that the reader can follow the meaning clearly. All except the most difficult words will be spelled correctly. Handwriting will be regular and well-formed.

Typical remarks in a level 6 answer:

From the point of view of a dog-lover, there is no doubt that the trouble that has to be taken in looking after a dog is more than worth it.

Walking him at least twice a day in all weathers, brushing him when he is losing his coat, bathing him when he is dirty or hot or when he might have fleas: these are among the most exhilarating pleasures of life. No dog owner looks on them as demands grudgingly carried out. They are routines affectionately indulged in so that the owner can show his or her love for man's best friend.

How to improve your level

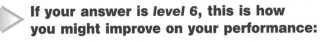

If your answer is *level* 6, this is how you might improve on your performance:

1 Alternate long and short sentences to give the best effect. Within the long sentences, do all you can to make sure there is a pleasant rhythm to your writing which will please the reader.

2 Try to get some real spirit into your writing by thinking of unusual ways of looking at the usual ideas.

3 Still search for the largest number of exact words. Think of different ways of expressing each idea that you have in mind and then pick the best words and phrases, those that exactly fit what you want to say.

How well did you do?

Level 7
26–33 marks

A level 7 answer will be, above all, well-planned. There will be a confidence and assurance about the expression. Words and phrases will be precisely chosen from a wide range of vocabulary. There will be a variety in the sentence structure so that the reader can easily follow the line of thought. Spelling and punctuation will be very accurate and handwriting will be clear and attractive.

Typical remarks in a level 7 answer:

Companionship, fun and healthy exercise are just some of the rewards experienced by any dog owner.
Exercise has to be taken routinely and energetically; food has to be bought and provided regularly; coats have to be bathed, groomed and kept in good condition. But all this loving attention is given freely and willingly.
Nothing can match the bond between person and dog. A loving trust on the one hand, and a sense of affectionate responsibility on the other, are two aspects of an enduring happiness and fulfilment that enrich the lives of thousands of people.

Where to find more help

Collins KS3 English Total Revision has several units on 'Imaginative Writing':

Level 4 pages 7–9

Level 5 pages 26–30

Level 6 pages 48–52

Level 7 pages 69–72

The chapter on 'The Essentials of Language' (pages 101–118) explains how to improve grammar, punctuation and spelling.

Test practice on Paper 1 Section C is on page 129; sample students' answers and examiner's comments are on pages 162–180.

Additional Paper 1
Section C Question 4(b)

Level 4
8–12 marks

Stories, especially those where you are given the beginning, are always the most popular writing tasks on Test papers. This is because they seem to be easy and give a chance for the writer to use his or her imagination to describe exciting events. However, at level 4, the writer will usually race on through one or two vivid events, not bothering to fill out the story with dialogue or detail, not searching for exact descriptive words and often being inconsistent with tenses. In fact, the style will be colloquial – that is, writing as you would speak.

Mostly, the writing will be in correct sentences, but punctuation and spelling may be poor, because the writer is in a hurry and does not check his or her expression.

Typical remarks in a level 4 answer:

When I hear this noise, I am walking round the top part of my estate and I can't make out where it is coming from. There is no-one on the street, so I go peering down the passages between the houses. I saw one with the back door open and a light on and then I heard another groan and the voice calling again. I was pretty scared. I thought I'd better go and see, so slowly I went down the passageway and saw this old woman on the ground. She told me she had come out and fallen down, so could I help her.

▷ **If your answer is *level 4*, this is how you might improve on your performance:**

1 You must be consistent with your tenses. If you start with the present tense, keep to it. If you start with the past tense, then stay with that.

2 Do not get so excited by your story that you let your sentences run on until they are too long and incorrect. Try to have some short sentences mixed in with longer ones. Do not use the word 'so' to connect long phrases to make them into sentences: this is not correct grammar.

3 Try to choose exact words to express your ideas and do not write in the same style in which you would speak: instead of phrases like 'make out' and 'pretty scared' use words like 'identify' and 'frightened'.

4 Use dialogue (speech) where you can. It breaks up the narrative and makes it seem more real.

How well did you do?

Level 5   *14–18 marks*

In a good level 5 story, the style will no longer be colloquial (written as if you are speaking), and the writer will search for more exact words and more accurate expression. Tenses will be consistent. It is natural to tell a story in the past tense and it is correct to do this even if the introduction has been in the present tense – provided you stick to the past tense. A level 5 story will include more details than a level 4 one.

Speech will be used, because this always adds a sense of drama and realism. Spelling and punctuation, including full stops, will be correct, and handwriting will usually be clear.

Typical remarks in a level 5 answer:

The old lady explained that she had come outside to investigate an unusual noise and now had fallen down and could not get up.

'Could you help me to get up?' she asked. 'Be careful, though, because I have fallen awkwardly and there's a sharp pain in my hip.'

My house was not far away, and so I told the lady that I would go home and fetch my mum or dad to see to her.

'Well, the trouble is that my little dog came out with me and now he's run off,' she said. 'Could you find him?'

How to improve your level

▷ **If your answer is *level 5*, this is how you might improve on your performance:**

1 Further develop the dialogue which you will already be using at level 5. Use it to control the speed of the story. Make it natural and make it fit the character who speaks it.

2 At points where you have intense feeling in your story, use description of some details at the scene. By writing in this direct, vivid way, you will concentrate the feeling in the mind of the reader.

3 Continue to search for precise words to give exact information and a good tone to your story. In our level 6 example (page 83), words like 'hurriedly', 'urgency', 'grabbed', 'tour' and 'traffic hazard' are not long or difficult words, but they express exactly the feeling that the writer wanted to put into the mind of the reader.

4 Check spelling, punctuation and sentence construction to make sure there are no irritating errors to interrupt the flow of the story.

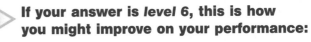

How well did you do?

Level 6
20–24 marks

At this level, dialogue and detail will be present through all the narrative – to give interest, to cause a change of pace, and to make it believable. A wider choice of words will be used and the words chosen will be more exact and will allow more thought and ideas to be included in the sentences. Spelling, punctuation and sentence construction will be almost entirely correct.

Typical remarks in a level 6 answer:

I rushed home and hurriedly told my parents about the old lady.

'You'd both better go,' I gasped. 'It'll be difficult to lift her up, and I think she might have broken her leg or hip.'

They set off with some urgency, while I reached for a torch , grabbed my bike, and pedalled off down the road. It was my intention to tour the district searching for a little, lost, itinerant dog. I desperately hoped to find him before he became a traffic hazard.

How to improve your level

▷ **If your answer is *level 6*, this is how you might improve on your performance:**

1 An intelligent reader will follow the rhythm of the sentences, and you need to make it easy for him or her by varying the length of the sentences from short and sharp, to long and detailed.

2 Find the most precise words for description of detail. Detail, if used sparingly, concentrates the mind of the reader and is most important in good story-writing. In our level 7 example (page 84), 'a whimpering, bedraggled scrap of fur' gives lots of detail about the distressed dog.

3 The end of a story must leave a satisfying, pleasant feeling in the mind of the reader – especially an examiner! Try to make the last few sentences either reflect back on what has gone before, or neatly round off something you have been leading up to.

How well did you do?

Level 7 *26–33 marks*

All the most developed elements of the craft of story-writing will now be present: variation of sentence structure, crisp and informative dialogue, use of significant detail as a focus for emotion. At the highest level, there will be a good use of suspense as a device for holding the attention of the reader. Handwriting will be perfectly clear, and spelling and punctuation will be faultless.

Typical remarks in a level 7 answer:

After I had searched in vain for the dog for half an hour, he arrived back at the lady's house on his own – a whimpering, bedraggled scrap of fur, unable to tell us about the lady's accident or his own perilous adventures. Meanwhile, my parents had raised the old lady and had got her fairly comfortably installed in her house. This was a difficult manoeuvre, hampered by shrieks from the lady, who was suffering excruciating pain in her hip.

'Some people passing by on the road gave us a most penetrating stare,' said Dad. 'I don't think they were sure whether we were good Samaritans or burglars!'

Where to find more help

Collins KS3 English Total Revision has several units on 'Imaginative Writing':

Level 4 pages 7–9

Level 5 pages 26–30

Level 6 pages 48–52

Level 7 pages 69–72

The chapter on 'The Essentials of Language' (pages 101–118) explains how to improve grammar, punctuation and spelling.

Test practice on Paper 1 Section C is on page 129; sample students' answers and examiner's comments are on pages 162–180.

Additional Paper 1
Section C Question 4(c)

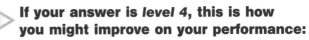

Level 4

8–12 marks

This task is a 'discursive' task – that is, you have to argue a case. Such tasks tend to be the least popular in tests because they are, in some ways, the hardest. This task asks you to write a letter and the question tells you how to set it out – remember to put the sender's address in the top right-hand corner, without your name on top. There are no special marks for setting out the letter, but it may count in overall structure.

A level 4 answer may be full of feeling, but may not be good in terms of organising the arguments which are suggested in the question. This is why argument is difficult: it is so much a matter of organisation. A level 4 answer will not contain paragraphs. The writer may be so carried away by feelings that he or she does not bother to search for exact words to describe those feelings. The style may be colloquial – that is, writing as you speak. Punctuation and spelling will be poor because the writer does not check his or her expression.

Typical remarks in a level 4 answer:

> *I am sick of all these people who go on about how terrible cars are, and how they make traffic jams and pollution and kill and injure people. I am a young mother who has to stay at home all day while my husband goes to work. I have to do four journeys taking my kids to school and back every day, and we need so many groceries that I couldn't carry them all from the shops without the car. Anyway, without the car I would spend all day walking backwards and forwards to the school and the shops.*

If your answer is *level 4*, this is how you might improve on your performance:

1 Do not let your sentences become too long because of the force of feeling that you are trying to convey. Our example has only four sentences, although it is a fair length, because it is running on in the manner of speech. It should have more and shorter sentences.

2 Do not write in the same style in which you would speak. Instead of 'sick', 'go on' and 'kids', use 'tired', 'complain' and 'children' – they are ordinary, but better, words.

3 Write in paragraphs. This is especially necessary in this kind of question, to show up the development of your argument.

How well did you do?

Level 5   *14–18 marks*

In a level 5 answer, the writing will no longer be colloquial (that is, written as if you are speaking). Sentences will be mostly correct, with full stops in the right places. In a letter, you will normally write in the present tense. The ideas will be arranged in paragraphs according to the suggestions in the question. Spelling, except for really difficult words, will be mostly correct. Punctuation, including full stops, capital letters, commas and apostrophes, will be mostly accurate and handwriting will be clear. A reasonable, though not very successful, attempt will be made to search for the most exact words to express the ideas the writer has.

Typical remarks in a level 5 answer:

> *I would like to support the view that cars are a great benefit to a great number of people, and I cannot understand why there are so many articles written about banning or restricting them.*
>
> *I know they may be dangerous when they are driven too fast, and they jam up town centres and pollute the air. But where would I be without a car to transport the children safely to school and other places they need to go? They don't seem to be safe walking about the streets on their own these days, and so I would rather take them and fetch them.*
>
> *Another point is that I have elderly parents, and if I didn't go and take them out shopping on Fridays, they would hardly get out of the house at all. I just could not do without my car.*

How to improve your level

▷ **If your answer is *level 5*, this is how you might improve on your performance:**

1 Try to find the most exact words for expressing your opinion: never be satisfied with the first form of expression you think of.

2 You may occasionally put in questions in this kind of writing. They are effective because the reader feels directly challenged. Usually, the answer to the question is obvious – these are called 'rhetorical' questions.

3 Check spelling, punctuation and sentence construction: these control the meaning as well as the individual words, and they must be accurate.

How well did you do?

Level 6 *20–24 marks*

In a level 6 answer the ideas will be well-organised in clear paragraphs. The paragraphs themselves, and the sentences within the paragraphs, will have a variety of well-controlled structures. There will be a strong, coherent argument running through the whole text of the letter. There will be a constant search for the best words and phrases to express the ideas. Punctuation will be accurate so that it makes the meaning clear, and all except the most difficult words will be spelled correctly.

Typical remarks in a level 6 answer:

> *Why do we have to be always blaming and obstructing and penalising the motorist? Most of the money spent on petrol goes to the government in tax, and after struggling for years to buy a car, the motorist is then blamed for pollution, traffic jams and dangers to pedestrians.*
>
> *We should admit that without the motor car, modern life as it is lived today would not be possible. Journeys to work, school, shops, entertainment, sport and all sorts of other activities – we need the car for all these things, and without it we could not do most of them.*
>
> *I ask that we stop complaining about the greatest asset to modern living.*

How to improve your level

▷ **If your answer is *level* 6, this is how you might improve on your performance:**

1 Vary your sentences. In this task, you are trying to persuade, and you can emphasise different ideas by where you place them in the sentence. Alternate long and short sentences for effect.

2 Plan your writing carefully before you start, so that your paragraphs will be clear and so that they will be arranged in the most effective order.

3 Try to make your writing come to a convincing conclusion, as if everything else has led up to it. Short sentences are often good for this, or sentences which quickly sum up the thoughts which have gone before.

How well did you do?

Level 7   *26–33 marks*

The argument will be forceful, convincing and eloquent. The paragraphs will be well-planned, clearly showing the different stages in the development of the writer's opinion. There will be a variation in sentence structure. The words and phrases will be precisely chosen from a wide range of vocabulary. Spelling and punctuation will be very accurate. Handwriting will be clear, attractive and regularly formed.

Typical remarks in a level 7 answer:

Life is full of contradictions. People nowadays enjoy the highest standard of living ever, and yet they are constantly complaining about the means needed to achieve that standard.

We have to allow that the car contributes its share of the pollution that is warming the world's climate, that it crowds and congests town and city centres everywhere, that it is lethal to drivers and pedestrians if not controlled properly. Surely, though, we must also concede that the motor car represents the greatest advance of all time in the technology which gives us our quality of life today.

Freedom of mobility is what everyone wants, and only the private car gives that. Employment, education, sport, entertainment, social activity: these are what everyone needs, and they are made possible by the motor car.

We must accept some of the costs if we are to continue to enjoy these huge benefits.

Where to find more help

Collins KS3 English Total Revision has several units on 'Writing to Inform and Persuade':

Level 4 pages 10–12

Level 5 pages 31–33

Level 6 pages 53–55

Level 7 pages 73–76

The chapter on 'The Essentials of Language' (pages 101–118) explains how to improve grammar, punctuation and spelling.

Test practice on Paper 1 Section C is on page 129; sample students' answers and examiner's comments are on pages 162–180.